WILD GAME
and
COUNTRY COOKING

by
TIMOTHY MANION

Recipes for the
Sportsman and Gourmet

ACKNOWLEDGEMENTS

Sincere thanks to the many who contributed their time and effort in making this book become a reality. Special people deserve mentioning for their support. Peg Proft whose encouragement and support helped me to finally finish this project. Melody Hughes for her ongoing support and unfailing devotion to completing a quality project, and of course to Diane Sprenger for her inspirational ability to organize and motivate, all with an unfailing sense of humor through adversity. My love and appreciation goes out to Barbara Manion Platt for her artistic input and love that you can only receive from a sister that is dear to you. And finally my mother who taught me at an early age the fun of cooking.

Copyright © 1983 by Timothy E. Manion

Compiled, published and edited by Manion Outdoors Co.

ISBN: 0-9612936-0-8

INTRODUCTION

This book is dedicated to my family and especially my father, who has given me a love and appreciation for nature and a strong sense of independence, to taste, smell and touch the finer things in life.

To write a cookbook is truly a self-indulgent pleasure of combining my two greatest loves; the outdoors and the creation of culinary delights.

This Wildgame Cookbook is the result of hearing many stories of the deer hunter, duck hunter or fisherman bringing home his proudly begotten game and having family not knowing how to prepare it.

Wildgame has a variety of tastes and qualities not found in beef and poultry. To bring out these delicate individual flavors, they have to be treated tenderly from the time you bag your quarry until the time it is served.

In this book, you will find a true appreciation for the individual preparation of each dish.

To enjoy fine food is one of man's greatest pleasures.

Fine food is created with a flair of imagination, a pinch of salt, and patience for perfection.

Today there exists a new generation of gourmets, many thousands of Americans who have enriched and nourished their lives through the Art of Gastronomy who have a deep appreciation for fine food and take pride and pleasure in preparing it.

To enjoy and prepare Walleye freshly caught, Pheasant Tarragon, or Barbecued Venison Rib Steaks sizzling on the grill is a mouth watering experience.

With literally millions of people who hunt and fish, there has been a steady growth and interest in more and better methods of preparing fish and game. In this book, you will discover recipes made easy for everyone to enjoy.

Let this first edition of **Wildgame and Country Cooking** benefit all my fellow sportsmen who enjoy the challenge of the stalk, the tranquility of nature and preparing a fine meal.

TABLE OF CONTENTS

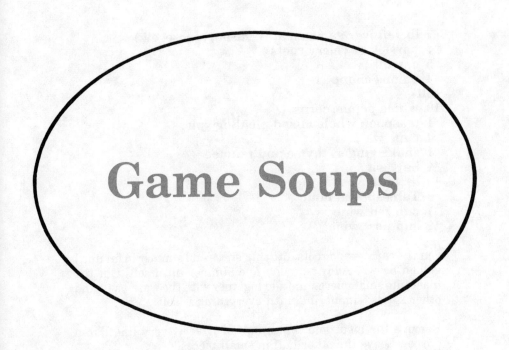

Game Soups

Game Soup A La Diane

A hearty main meal

¾ lb. leftover game meat (venison, moose, elk)
4 parsley or celery roots
5 carrots
4 onions chopped
salt
10 whole peppercorns
1 teaspoon whole mixed pickling spices
4 cups water
1 shake ginger, thyme and nutmeg
½ bay leaf
¼ lb. butter
4 Tablespoons flour
1 cup red wine
½ cup port wine

Cut the carrots and roots into thin slices and simmer in fat until golden brown. Add the onion and simmer until soft. Cut the meat into small pieces and add together with the water, salt and other spices; simmering until everything is soft.

Remove the meat and mince half of it very, very fine like a puree´. Leave the other half in small pieces.

Mix flour with a little water and add to the other ingredients in the pot. Boil for at least 30 minutes over moderate heat. Now pour it through a sieve, pour in the red wine, the port wine and cream. Heat — but do not boil — then put the meat pieces and the meat puree´ back in and serve immediately.

Makes 6-8 servings.

Cheese Smothered Onion Soup

3 large onions thinly sliced
2 ounces of cooking sherry
1 clove garlic - minced
¼ cup vegetable stock or browned beef stock
4 thick slices French bread
4 ounces Swiss or Gruyere cheese sliced
grated Parmesan cheese

In covered saucepan cook onions and garlic in butter over low heat 20 minutes or until very tender; stir occasionally. Add stock, ¼ teaspoon pepper and sherry. Bring to boiling; cover and simmer 15 minutes. Meanwhile, toast bread. Ladle soup into four soup bowls top with toasted bread and cheese then put under the broiler 2-3 minutes or until cheese melts. Top with Parmesan cheese.

Makes 4 servings.

Captain Jack Chowder

1 cup chopped red onion
1 Tablespoon soy sauce
1 teaspoon dried thyme
2 Tablespoons butter
¼ cup parsley - fresh
½ teaspoon salt
1 bay leaf
dash bottled hot pepper sauce
1 pinch shredded oysters
2 cups milk
½ cup light cream
2 cups shredded American cheese - yield 8 ounces
½ cup dry white wine

In saucepan cook onion and parsley in butter until onion is tender. Stir in soy, thyme, salt, bay leaf, and pepper sauce. Add undrained oysters; cook and stir over medium heat 5 minutes or until edges of oysters curl. Stir in milk and cream; heat through. Stir in cheese until melted. Remove from heat; stir in wine. Remove bay leaf.

Makes 6 servings.

Shrimp Bisque
An absolute scrumptious meal in itself

1 **lemon cut in wedges**
1 **cup diced potatoes**
2 **cups milk**
¾ **cups chopped onion**
1 **cup chopped celery**
2 **Tablespoons butter**
10 **ounces fresh boiled shrimp**
2 **Tablespoons all purpose flour**

In saucepan combine celery, potatoes, onion, 1 cup water, ½ teaspoon salt and dash pepper. Bring to boiling. Reduce heat; cover and simmer 15 minutes or until potatoes are tender, stirring occasionally. Blend milk and flour; stir into potato mixture. Add shrimp and butter. Cook and stir until thickened and bubbly. Garnish with snipped parsley if desired and freshly squeezed lemon.

Makes 4 servings.

Sheepshead Stew

2 lb. fresh dressed sheepshead (trim away belly meat and discard)
2 cups water
⅓ cup snipped parsley
4 cloves garlic
½ teaspoon salt
1 medium onion sliced
1 stalk celery, sliced - yield ½ cup
2 Tablespoons olive oil
2 medium potatoes, peeled and sliced
2 large carrots, sliced - yield 1 cup
3 tomatoes peeled and cubed
1 teaspoon salt
¼ teaspoon pepper

Remove skin from fish. In 10 inch skillet combine fish, water, parsley, garlic and the ½ teaspoon salt. Bring mixture to boiling. Reduce heat; cover and simmer gently about 2-3 minutes or until fish flakes easily when tested with a fork.

In 4 quart dutch oven cook onion and celery in hot oil until vegetables are tender but not brown. Add potatoes and carrots, cook and stir until lightly browned. Stir in tomatoes, the 1 teaspoon salt and the pepper. Strain stock from fish; discard parsley and garlic. Add stock to dutch oven. Bring to boiling. Reduce heat, cover pan tightly and simmer about 30 minutes or until vegetables are tender. Meanwhile, remove and discard bones from fish; break fish into chunks. Add fish to vegetables mixture; heat through.

Makes 6 servings.

O'Mannion Irish Stew

1 lb. boneless lamb, cut into 1 inch cubes
1 medium onion cut into thin wedges
1 bay leaf
1½ teaspoon salt
¼ teaspoon pepper
2 medium potatoes peeled and thinly sliced - yield 2 cups
1 medium turnip peeled and chopped - yield 1 cup
1 9-ounce package frozen cut green beans
1 Tablespoon snipped parsley
¼ teaspoon dried basil
¼ teaspoon dried oregano crushed

In large saucepan or dutch oven combine lamb, onion, bay leaf, salt and pepper. Add 4 cups water. Bring to boiling. Reduce heat; cover and simmer for 1 hour. Stir in potatoes, turnip, green beans, parsley, basil and oregano. Cover and cook 25-30 minutes more or until vegetables are tender. Remove bay leaf. Season to taste.

Makes 6 servings.

Zesty Polish Chowder

1 lb. fully cooked Polish sausage cut into ½ inch pieces
    2 medium potatoes peeled and chopped - yield 2 cups
    1 medium onion chopped - yield ½ cup
1½ teaspoon salt
dash pepper
    2 cups water
    1 small head cabbage shredded - yield 4 cups
    3 cups milk
    3 Tablespoons all purpose flour
    1 cup shredded Swiss cheese - yield 4 ounces
snipped parsley

In large saucepan or dutch oven combine sausage, potatoes, onions, salt and pepper. Add water. Bring to boil, reduce heat; cover and simmer 20 minutes or until vegetables are tender. Stir in 2½ cups of the milk. Blend remaining ½ cup milk and flour; stir into soup. Cook and stir till thickened and bubbly. Stir in cheese until melted. Garnish with parsley.

Makes 6 servings.

Venison Sausage - Vegetable Chowder

2 Tablespoons butter
3 Tablespoons all purpose flour
1 teaspoon salt
1 teaspoon onion powder
¼ teaspoon dried dill weed
⅛ teaspoon pepper
4 cups milk
1 10-ounce package frozen vegetables, partially thawed (lima beans, cauliflower, green beans, peas and carrots or broccoli)
1 16-ounce can whole kernel corn, drained
12 ounces venison sausage or smoked sausage links sliced

In a large saucepan melt butter over low heat. Blend in flour, salt, onion powder, dill weed and pepper. Add milk all at once. Cook over medium heat, stirring constantly until thickened and bubbly. Cut the partially thawed frozen vegetables into bite size pieces if necessary. Stir the vegetables, corn and sausage into the soup. Cover and simmer for 10-15 minutes or until vegetables are done.

Makes 6 servings.

Chunky Ham and Pea Soup

2 11¼-ounce cans condensed green pea soup
1 cup chicken broth
2 cups milk
1 6¾ ounce can chunk style ham, drained and diced or 1
   cup diced fully cooked ham
3 ounces freshly sliced mushrooms
¼ cup dry white wine

In saucepan combine pea soup and chicken broth; cook and stir in milk. Cook and stir until heated through. Stir in ham, undrained mushrooms and wine; heat through.

Makes 4-6 servings.

Ranchhand Soup

3 cups coarsely chopped cabbage
1 medium onion chopped - yield 1½ cups
2 cups water
1 17-ounce can lima beans
1 11½-ounce can condensed bean with bacon soup
1 Tablespoon prepared mustard
1 12-ounce can corned beef, chilled and diced

In saucepan simmer cabbage and onion in the water, covered for 8-10 minutes or until tender. Stir in the undrained bean soup and mustard. Stir in corned beef; heat through.

Serves 4-6.

South of the Border Bean Soup

½ cup chopped onion
1 clove garlic minced
2 Tablespoons cooking oil
2 16-ounce cans red kidney beans drained
1 16-ounce can cream style corn
1 4-ounce can green chili peppers, rinsed, seeded and chopped
1 Tablespoon instant chicken bouillon
1 teaspoon ground cumin
Puffy cheese noodles

In 5 quart dutch oven cook onion and garlic in oil till onion is tender. Stir in next 6 ingredients, 6 cups water, 2 teaspoons salt and ¼ teaspoon pepper. Cover and simmer 25 minutes. Add puffy cheese noodles; simmer uncovered 10-12 minutes or until noodles are done.

Serves 6-8.

Aunt Nevada's Chicken Soup

    6 cups water
    1 5-6 lb. stewing chicken cut up
 1/3 cup chopped onion
    2 teaspoons salt
 1/4 teaspoon pepper
    1 bay leaf
    1 16-ounce can cream style corn
    2 small zucchini thinly sliced - yield 2 cups
1 1/2 cups uncooked homemade noodles

In a large kettle combine water, chicken pieces, chopped onion, salt, pepper and bay leaf. Bring to boil, reduce heat. Cover and simmer about 2 hours or until chicken is tender. Remove chicken from broth. Skim fat from broth; remove bay leaf. When chicken is cool enough to handle, remove skin and bones from chicken, discard. Cube chicken; set aside.

Add undrained tomatoes; cream style corn and thinly sliced zucchini to broth. Bring mixture to boiling. Stir in homemade noodles. Cover and simmer about 8 minutes or until noodles are nearly tender. Stir in the cubed chicken. Cover and simmer about 5 minutes more or until heated through. Season to taste with salt and pepper.

Makes 8 servings.

Squirrel Brunswick Stew

 1 2½-3 lb. squirrel cut up
 6 cups water
1½ teaspoons salt
 1 teaspoon dried rosemary
 1 bay leaf
 2 medium potatoes peeled and diced - yield 2 cups
 1 16-ounce can tomatoes cut up
 1 16-ounce can cream style corn
 1 10-ounce package frozen cut okra
 1 10-ounce package frozen lima beans
 1 large onion chopped - yield 1 cup
 1 Tablespoon sugar
1½ teaspoon salt
 ½ teaspoon pepper

Place meat in 5 quart dutch oven. Add water, 1½ teaspoon salt, rosemary and bay leaf. Bring to boiling. Reduce heat; cover and simmer about 1 hour or until squirrel is tender. Remove meat from broth. Skim fat from broth. When squirrel is cool enough to handle, remove bones from the squirrel and discard bones. Cut up meat. Return to broth. Stir in potatoes, undrained tomatoes, corn, okra, beans, onions, sugar, 1½ teaspoon salt and pepper. Cover and simmer 40 minutes. Remove bay leaf.

Makes 8-10 servings.

Pheasant Chowder
An elegant soup delicious with a hearty burgundy

1 medium onion chopped - yield ½ cup
¼ cup butter
¼ cup all purpose flour
½ teaspoon seasoned salt
¼ teaspoon ground pepper
3 cups chicken broth
5 medium cucumbers about 2 lb. peeled
2 cups cubed boiled pheasant or white breasted bird
½ cup long grain rice
2 Tablespoons lemon juice
2 bay leaves
1 cup light cream
¼ cup snipped parsley

In 3 quart saucepan, cook onion in butter until tender but not brown. Blend in flour, seasoned salt, and ground pepper. Stir in chicken broth. Cook and stir until thickened and bubbly. Add cucumbers. Cover and simmer for 10 minutes. Pour half the mixture at a time into blender container. Cover and blend on medium speed for 30 seconds. Return all to saucepan.

Stir in pheasant, uncooked rice, lemon juice and bay leaves. Return to boiling. Reduce heat, cover and simmer 20 to 25 minutes or until rice is tender. Remove bay leaves. Stir in cream and parsley; heat through. Season to taste. Garnish with fresh parsley.

Makes 6 servings.

Hearty Vegetable Soup

4 cups beef broth
1 16-ounce can garbanzo beans drained
1 16-ounce can tomatoes cut up
1 8-ounce can cut green beans drained
½ cup shell macaroni
½ cup chopped onion
½ cup finely chopped carrot
½ teaspoon dried basil crushed
¼ teasoon dried rosemary
¼ teaspoon dried thyme

In 4 quart dutch oven, combine all ingredients. Cover and simmer 30-40 minutes or till vegetables are tender.

Makes 8 servings.

Old Fashioned Borscht

4 cups browned beef stock
4 medium beets, peeled and cubed - yield 3 cups
2 medium carrots chopped - yield 1 cup
1 medium onion chopped - yield ½ cup
1 bay leaf
1 Tablespoon vinegar
1 teaspoon sugar
1 teaspoon salt
¼ teaspoon ground pepper
½ small head cabbage shredded - yield 3 cups
1 16-ounce can tomatoes cut up
2 slightly beaten egg yolks
½ cup dairy sour cream

In a 4 quart dutch oven combine browned beef stock or vegetable stock, beets, carrots, onion, bay leaf, vinegar, sugar, salt and pepper. Bring to boiling — reduce heat; cover and simmer for 40 minutes. Stir in cabbage and undrained tomatoes. Cover and cook 30-35 minutes more or until vegetables are tender. Remove bay leaf.

Blend egg yolks and sour cream; gradually stir in about 1 cup of the hot mixture. Return to dutch oven; heat through, stirring constantly over low heat. Do not boil. Serve immediately.

Makes 6-8 servings.

Fresh Mushroom Barley Soup

8 ounces fresh mushrooms sliced - yield 3 cups
1 medium green pepper chopped - yield ½ cup
1 medium onion chopped - yield ½ cup
1 clove garlic minced
2 Tablespoons butter
¾ cup quick cooking barley
¾ teaspoon ground sage
½ teaspoon salt
5 cups beef broth

In 3 quart covered saucepan cook mushrooms, green pepper, onion and garlic in butter about 5 minutes or until tender but not brown. Stir in barley, sage and salt. Add broth; bring to boiling. Reduce heat; cover and simmer 20-25 minute or until barley is tender.

Makes 6 servings.

Spinach-Cheddar Cheese Soup

½ cup chopped onion
½ cup chopped celery
¼ cup butter
¼ cup all purpose flour
½ teaspoon pepper
4 cups milk
1 10-ounce package frozen chopped spinach
1½ cups shredded medium cheddar cheese

In 3 quart saucepan cook onion and celery in butter or margarine till onion is tender. Stir in flour, salt and pepper. Add milk all at once; cook and stir until thickened and bubbly. Stir in spinach and cheese; cook and stir until cheese melts.

Makes 4 to 6 servings.

Orchard Soup

  1 small butternut squash halved and seeded -
      yield 16 ounces
  3 medium green apples peeled, cored and coarsely
      chopped - yield 3 cups
  2 10¾ ounce cans condensed chicken broth
1½ cups water
  3 slices white bread torn into pieces
  1 medium onion, chopped - yield ½ cup
  1 teaspoon salt
 ¼ teaspoon dried rosemary
 ¼ teasoon freshly ground pepper
 ¼ teaspoon dried marjoram
 ¼ cup whipping cream
snipped parsley

Peel and cut up squash. In 4 quart dutch oven combine the squash, apples, condensed chicken broth, water, bread, onion, salt, rosemary, marjoram and pepper. Bring to boiling. Reduce heat; simmer uncovered for 45 minutes. Turn one fourth of the soup mixture into a blender container. Cover and blend till smooth; set aside. Repeat with remaining mixture, one fourth at a time. Then return all the soup to the dutch oven. Bring to boiling. Reduce heat to simmer. Stir in cream. Garnish each serving with snipped parsley.

Makes 6-8 servings.

Peanut Butter Chowder

2 cups water
1 envelope regular chicken noodle soup mix
1 Tablespoon finely chopped onion
¼ teaspoon salt
2 cups milk
1 16-ounce can cream style corn
2 Tablespoons creamy style peanut butter

In 3 quart saucepan bring water to boiling; add soup mix, onion, and salt. Reduce heat; cover and simmer about 10 minutes or until noodles are tender. Stir in milk, corn and peanut butter, heat through.

Makes 4-6 servings.

Wild Asparagus Soup

Wild asparagus can be picked along
country fence rows in late May

¾ lb. asparagus cut up or 1 10-ounce package frozen cut
    asparagus
1 thin slice onion
½ cup boiling water
1 cup milk
½ cup light cream

In covered saucepan cook asparagus and onion slice in water 8-10 minutes or until crisp - tender do not drain. Cool slightly. In blender container or food processor, combine the undrained asparagus and onion, milk, cream, ½ teaspoon salt and dash pepper. Cover and blend until smooth. Chill for 3-4 hours. Stir or blend before serving.

Makes 4-6 servings.

Venison Cider Stew

2 lbs. venison stew meat, cut into 1 inch cubes
3 Tablespoons all purpoe flour
2 teaspoons salt
¼ teaspoon pepper
¼ teaspoon dried thyme
3 Tablespoons cooking oil
2 cups apple cider or apple juice
1-2 Tablespoons vinegar
3 potatoes peeled and quartered
4 carrots quartered
2 onions sliced
1 stalk celery sliced

Coat meat with mixture of flour, salt, pepper and thyme. In 4½ quart dutch oven brown meat, half at a time, in hot oil. Drain off fat. Return all meat to dutch oven. Stir in apple cider or juice, vinegar and ½ cup water, cook and stir until mixture boils. Reduce heat, cover and simmer about 1¼ hours or until meat is nearly tender. Stir in vegetables. Cook 30 minutes more or until vegetables are done.

Makes 6-8 servings.

Shiocton Beef and Sauerkraut Soup

2 lb. beef shank or venison shank crosscuts
2 Tablespoons cooking oil
1 medium onion chopped - yield ½ cup
1 clove garlic minced
4 whole cloves
1 bay leaf
1 teaspoon salt
⅛ teaspoon pepper
1 8-ounce can sauerkraut snipped
1 8-ounce can tomatoes cut up
1 medium apple peeled cored and chopped
1 green pepper chopped - yield ½ cup
1 teaspoon sugar

In dutch oven brown meat in hot oil, remove from pan; add onion and garlic to drippings and cook until onion is tender. Return beef to pan. Add cloves, bay leaf, salt, pepper and 4 cups water. Cover and simmer for 1½ hours. Remove beef. Remove bay leaf and cloves. When cool enough to handle, remove meat from bones; cut up meat and return to broth. Discard bones. Stir in undrained sauerkraut, undrained tomatoes, apple, green pepper and sugar. Bring to boiling; reduce heat. Cover and simmer 15-20 minutes more or until pepper is tender. Top with sour cream if desired.

Makes 6 servings.

Meatball Stew with Spinach Dumplings

1 beaten egg
¾ cups soft bread crumbs (1 slice)
1 teaspoon garlic salt
1 lb. ground venison
1 Tablespoon cooking oil
1 medium onion chopped - yield ½ cup
1 11-ounce can condensed Cheddar cheese soup
1 soup can milk - yield 1¼ cup
1 16-ounce can diced beets drained
1 10-ounce package frozen brussel sprouts
1 8-ounce can spinach well drained and chopped
1 cup packaged biscuit mix
¼ cup milk

Mix egg, crumbs and garlic salt. Add meat, mix well. Shape meat mixture into 1 inch meatballs. In 12 inch skillet, brown meatballs in hot oil. Add onion; cook 5 minutes. Drain off fat. Combine cheese soup and the soup can of milk; add to skillet. Cover and simmer 10 minutes. Add beets and sprouts. Cover and simmer 5 minutes. Stir together spinach, biscuit mix and the ¼ cup milk. Drop spinach mixture atop soup mixture to make eight dumplings. Cover simmer 10 minutes.

Makes 4 servings.

Ground Venison and Beer
Vegetable Soup

1 lb. ground venison
1 medium onion chopped - yield ½ cup
1 12-ounce can beer
1 10½-ounce can condensed beef broth
1 soup can water - yield 1¼ cup
3 medium carrots thinly sliced - yield 1½ cup
1 medium turnip chopped - yield 1 cup
1 stalk celery thinly sliced - yield ½ cup
1 4-ounce can mushroom stems and pieces
1 bay leaf
1 teaspoon salt
⅛ teaspoon pepper
⅛ teaspoon ground allspice

In large saucepan cook ground venison and onion until meat is browned; drain off fat. Stir in beer, condensed beef broth, water, carrots, turnip, celery, undrained mushrooms, bay leaf, salt, pepper and allspice. Bring to boiling. Reduce heat; cover and simmer for 30-35 minutes or until vegetables are tender. Remove bay leaf.

Makes 4-6 servings.

Farm Fresh Stew

12 chicken thighs, skinned - yield 3 lbs.
2 Tablespoons cooking oil
1 6-ounce envelope Italian salad dressing mix
1 teaspoon salt
3 cups water
½ cup dry white wine
½ cup catsup
3 medium potatoes peeled and cubed - yield 3 cups
2 cups frozen small whole onions - yield ½ of a 20 ounce package
1 10-ounce package frozen cut broccoli
1 medium green pepper cut into cubes
2 cups sliced fresh mushrooms - yield 5 ounces
⅓ cup cold water
3 Tablespoons all purpose flour

In 4½ quart dutch oven slowly brown chicken thighs, half at a time, in the hot oil. Remove chicken; drain fat from pan. In same dutch oven combine dry salad dressing mix and salt. Sir in the 3 cups water, wine and catsup. Return the browned chicken thighs to pan. Bring to boiling. Reduce heat; cover and simmer for 15 minutes.

Add potatoes and frozen onions. Simmer covered 15 minutes longer. Add frozen broccoli, the green pepper and mushrooms. Cover and simmer 5-10 minutes longer or until vegetables are tender. Blend the ⅓ cup cold water and the flour; stir into stew. Cook and stir until thickened and bubbly.

Makes 6 servings.

Simple White Wine Marinade

for fish fillets or steaks; small game birds

½ **cup dry vermouth or white wine**
¼ **cup olive oil**
Juice of one lemon
2 **Tablespoons fresh parsley, chopped**

Combine ingredients. Yields approximately 3/4 cup marinade. Increase according to needs. For an Italian herb marinade add fresh or dried basil, tarragon, rosemary, thyme, oregano, marjoram, and/or garlic.

Puréed Red Wine Marinade
for game meat; waterfowl

1 **large onion, peeled**
2 **cloves garlic, peeled**
½ **teaspoon salt**
½ **teaspoon pepper**
¼ **teaspoon cayenne pepper**
1 **bay leaf**
¼ **cup red wine vinegar**
½ **cup olive oil (or salad oil)**
1 **teaspoon Worcestershire sauce**

Coarsely chop onion and place in the body of a food processor or blender. Add the garlic, salt, pepper, cayenne, bay leaf, and wine vinegar. Blend to a smooth purée. Add the wine, oil and Worcestershire sauce and blend everything thoroughly. Approximate yield: 1¾ cups marinade. Cover food with marinade and refrigerate, according to recipe.

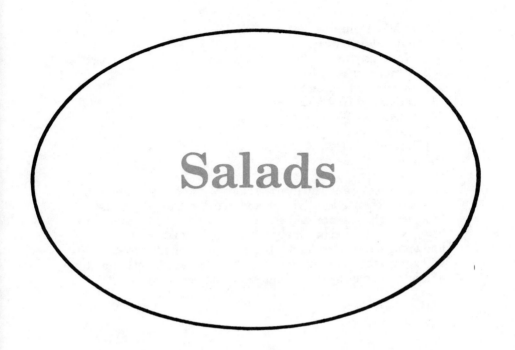

Salads

Caesar Salad
Delicious and a meal in itself

1½ **heads Romaine lettuce**
1 **egg (coddled)**
1 **clove garlic**
2 **ounces olive oil**
1 **ounce red vinegar**
¼ **teaspoon dry mustard**
¼ **teaspoon Worcestershire sauce**
1 **anchovy**
1 **lemon**
Parmesan cheese

Break up garlic and rub into the sides of a wood bowl along with anchovy. Then add olive oil and red vinegar, dry mustard, Worcestershire sauce and stir vigorously in the bottom of the bowl. Now, proceed in adding lettuce to the mixture. Coddle egg and break over lettuce and squeeze lemon over entire salad (this will counteract the bitterness of the lettuce). Toss thoroughly and add Parmesan cheese and serve immediately.

Makes 4 servings.

Gary Backes
Burlington, Wisconsin

Cobb Salad

½ head Bibb lettuce
½ head Romaine
1 small bunch of chicory
½ bunch watercress
1 small tomato
2 breasts of cooked partridge
6 slices bacon
3 peeled avocados
1 egg - hard boiled
2 Tablespoons chives

In salad bowl, mix lettuce, small chicory, watercress, tomato — all finely chopped. Toss the mixture thoroughly and sprinkle over it finely diced meat and bacon. Cut avocados in small pieces and arrange the pieces around the edge of the salad. Chop egg finely and sprinkle on salad. Add Blue Cheese Roquefort dressing and chives.

Makes 4 servings.

Wilted Dandelion Greens

1 quart coarsely shredded dandelion greens
4 strips bacon, diced
2 teaspoons sugar
½ teaspoon salt
Dash of freshly ground black pepper
¼ teaspoon dry mustard
3 Tablespoons mild vinegar

Tough roots or stems should be removed from the greens before shredding them. Place the greens in a large bowl. Cook the bacon until crisp. Add the remaining ingredients to the bacon and fat and heat, stirring, until the sugar has dissolved. Pour the mixture over the dandelion greens and toss well.

Makes 3-4 servings.

German Potato Salad
With Sour Cream

1 lb. potatoes, boiled (about 4 medium potatoes)
1 teaspoon sugar
½ teaspoon salt
¼ teaspoon dry mustard
⅛ teaspoon freshly ground black pepper
2 Tablespoons vinegar
1 cup sour cream
½ cup thinly sliced cucumbers (optional)
Paprika

Slice potatoes while still warm. If new potatoes are used, slice in their jackets. Old potatoes should be peeled.

Mix the sugar, salt, mustard, pepper and vinegar. Add the sour cream and cucumber and mix. Pour over the potatoes and toss lightly until all the potatoes have been coated with dressing. Turn into a serving dish and sprinkle with paprika. Serve warm or cool.

Makes 4 servings.

Coleslaw With Bacon

5 slices bacon
2 eggs
5 Tablespoons sugar
½ cup vinegar
½ cup water
1 teaspoon salt
½ cup heavy cream
1 head cabbage
1 hard boiled egg

In a skillet saute´ 5 slices of diced bacon until crisp. Reserve half the bacon bits. Beat 2 eggs and add to them 5 Tablespoons sugar, ½ cup each of vinegar and water, 1 teaspoon salt. Beat the mixture well and add it to the bacon and bacon fat in the skillet. Heat the mixture slowly and beat it until it thickens, being careful not to let it boil. Remove the skillet from the heat and stir in ½ cup heavy cream. Pour the dressing over 1 head of cabbage, finely sliced, toss it lightly and garnish with the reserved bacon and a little chopped hard cooked egg.

Chick Pea Salad

2 cups cooked or canned chick peas, drained
¼ cup chopped pimento
½ cup chopped green pepper
1 cup chopped celery
Salt and fresh ground black pepper to taste
½ - ¾ cup mayonnaise or salad dressing
2 - 3 Tablespoons prepared horseradish
Lettuce

Combine the chick peas, pimento, green pepper, celery, salt and pepper and toss lightly. Combine the mayonnaise and horseradish and stir gently into the mixture. Just before serving, arrange on crisp lettuce.

Makes 6-8 servings.

Kidney Bean and Egg Salad

  2 **cups canned kidney beans, drained**
  ½ **cup diced celery**
  ¼ **cup sweet pickle relish**
  2 **hard cooked eggs, sliced**
  1 **Tablespoon finely chopped onion**
French dressing to taste
Lettuce

Combine the kidney beans, celery, pickle relish, eggs and onion.
Pour dressing over the bean mixture and toss lightly. Chill
thoroughly and serve on crisp lettuce.

Makes 6 servings.

Betty's Pink Salad
A must for a summer picnic

1 large pkg. Philadelphia cream cheese
1 jar Maraschino cherries
1 small bag miniature marshmallows
1 large can crushed pineapple
1 envelope of Dream Whip

Mix up the cream cheese with the cherries in a bowl with a fork or whip at a low speed in the blender. Now add the crushed pineapple after draining off the juice. Prepare one envelope of Dream Whip and fold into mixture. Add marshmallows and refrigerate for at least two hours before serving.
Makes 6 servings.

Betty Manion
Hortonville, Wisconsin

Sunshine Salad

2 small packages (4 ounces each) orange jello
2 cups hot water, boiling
2 cans mandarin oranges, reserve juice
1 pint orange sherbet

Dissolve jello in 2 cups of boiling water. Add reserved mandarin orange juice. Let stand for 20 minutes. Stir in orange sections and the orange sherbet. Chill until set.

Makes 8 servings.

Cantaloupe Farmer's Style

2 cantaloupes
French dressing
1 large or 2 small cucumbers
Salt
½ cup sour cream
Lettuce leaves
Hard cooked egg slices (optional)

Cut the cantaloupes in half, peel and remove the seeds. Dice the meat and marinate in French dressing for half an hour in a cool place. Peel and finely slice the cucumber and sprinkle with salt. Let stand one hour. Drain the cantaloupe and cucumber thoroughly and mix with the sour cream. Arrange on crisp lettuce leaves and garnish with hard cooked eggs.

Makes 4-6 servings.

Vegetables, Casseroles and Stuffings

Tarte Aux Asperges
Asparagus Pie

        1 - 9" pie pastry
    2½ lbs. asparagus
        2 cups heavy cream
        6 whole peppercorns
        4 sprigs of parsley
        4 thin onion slices
        1 bay leaf
Thyme
Marjoram
        ½ cup grated Gruyere cheese
        ¾ cup bread crumbs
Butter

Cook asparagus tips, heat cream with peppercorns, parsley, onions, bay leaf, pinch of thyme, and a pinch of marjoram. Simmer mixture very gently for 15 minutes.

In a skillet sauté 1 Tablespoon butter with 3 Tablespoons chopped lean ham for 2 minutes, stirring constantly. Strain the hot cream and stir it gradually into the meat, continuing to stir until the sauce begins to boil. Lower the heat and simmer the sauce very gently, uncovered, for 30 minutes, stirring occasionally to prevent scorching.

Line the bottom of the pie shell with a layer of asparagus tips, arranging them so the points face toward the edge of the pie shell. Blend the remaining sauce with ½ cup grated Gruyere cheese and pour it over the top layer. Sprinkle the pie with ¾ cup fine bread crumbs and dot with bits of butter. Brown the topping quickly under the broiler. Serve the pie immediately.

Makes 4 servings.

Shrimp-Stuffed Artichokes

    4 medium artichokes
    1 cup cooked shrimp, shelled and deveined
 1½ cups soft bread crumbs
    ¼ cup finely chopped onion
    ½ teaspoon salt
Fresh lemon juice
    1 egg, beaten
Olive or salad oil

Prepare artichokes for stuffing. Preheat oven to 350°. Cut the shrimp into small pieces and combine with bread crumbs, onion, salt, two teaspoons of lemon juice and the egg. Spoon the mixture into the artichokes. Place them in a small baking pan and pour boiling water around them to the depth of 1". Add 1 Tablespoon lemon juice and brush the artichokes generously with olive or salad oil. Cover with aluminum foil and bake thirty minutes.

Artichoke Hearts vs Artichoke Bottoms: Artichoke hearts and bottoms are not the same. The heart (such as that purchased frozen) consists of a portion of the heart, the "choke" removed, and a few tender leaves. The bottom is precisely that. It is the bottom of the vegetable with all leaves and choke removed.

Makes 4 servings.

Chuck Wagon Baked Beans

2 cups navy beans
4 cups cold water
¼ pound piece of salt pork
½ salt pork
½ cup molasses
1 teaspoon grated onion
½ teaspoon mustard
¼ teaspoon paprika

Pick over navy beans and put them in a pot with cold water to soak overnight. The pot should be kept in a cool place. In the morning the beans should have absorbed the water. If any water remains, drain it off and reserve it. Add fresh cold water to cover and simmer the beans over low heat in a tightly covered pot for one hour. Drain the beans and reserve the water.

Put a ¼ pound piece of salt pork or fat bacon in the bottom of an earthenware bean pot and pour in the beans. Bury a second piece of salt pork and well scored, in the center. Mix together ½ each of molasses and reserved bean water, 1 scant teaspoon grated onion, dry mustard and paprika. Pour the mixture over the beans, lifting them carefully with a spoon so that the seasoning will penetrate to the bottom of the pot.

Cover the pot and bake the beans in a slow oven, 300° for six (6) hours. Once each hour add a little of the reserved bean water, again lifting the beans gently so that the water will sink to the bottom of the pot. The surface of the water in the pot should always be even with the beans. If there is too little water, the beans will become dry and hard rather than tender and mealy. During the last hour of cooking, remove the lid of the bean pot so that the pork on the surface will become crisp and brown.

Best In The West Beans

Molasses to taste
½ lb. ground beef
10 bacon slices, chopped
½ cup onion, chopped
¼ cup packed brown sugar
¼ cup granulated sugar
¼ cup catsup
¼ cup barbecue sauce
2 Tablespoons mustard
½ teaspoon salt
½ teaspoon chili powder
½ teaspoon pepper
1 16-ounce can kidney beans, drained
1 16-ounce can pork and beans
1 16-ounce can butter beans

Brown meats; drain. Add onion and cook until tender. Add combined sugars, catsup, barbecue sauce, mustard, molasses and seasonings, mix well. Add beans, pour into 3 quart casserole dish. Bake at 350° for one hour.

Makes 10-12 servings.

Peggy Proft
West Allis, Wisconsin

Company Broccoli

2 Tablespoons onion
2 Tablespoons butter
2 Tablespoons flour
1 teaspoon salt
2 packages (10 ounces each) frozen chopped broccoli
3 eggs beaten
1 cup sharp cheddar cheese, grated
½ cup bread crumbs
¼ cup sliced almonds

Brown the onions and butter for 5 minutes. Blend in the flour
and salt. Cook the broccoli as directed on the package; drain.
Beat 3 eggs and add to the flour mixture. Mix with the drained
broccoli. Blend in shredded cheese and bread crumbs. Turn into
buttered casserole dish and sprinkle almonds on top. Bake at
350° approximately 50 minutes until set.

Makes 8 servings.

Sour Cream Sauce For Broccoli And Cashews

2 Tablespoons minced onion
2 Tablespoons butter
1½ cup sour cream
1 teaspoon honey
1 teaspoon cider vinegar
½ teaspoon poppy seed
½ teaspoon paprika
¼ teaspoon salt
⅓ cup chopped cashews
Dash cayenne
2½ to 3 cups cooked, drained broccoli

Sauté onions in butter in a saucepan; add sour cream, honey, vinegar, poppy seed, paprika, salt and cayenne. Heat carefully until hot. Serve on cooked, drained broccoli. Garnish with cashews.

Makes 4 servings.

Mexican-Style Cauliflower

1 medium head of cauliflower, separated into flowerets
1½ cups tomato sauce
2 Tablespoons chopped parsley
⅛ teaspoon cloves
¼ teaspoon cinnamon
1 Tablespoon capers
2 Tablespoons chopped olives
3 Tablespoons grated cheese
2 Tablespoons fine bread crumbs
1 Tablespoon olive or salad oil

Preheat oven to 425°. Cook the flowerets, covered, in a small amount of boiling salted water until barely tender. Drain. Mix the tomato sauce, parsley, spices, capers, and olives. Pour a little of the sauce into a heatproof baking dish, add cauliflower, and cover with remaining sauce. Sprinkle with the cheese, crumbs and oil and bake until brown.

Makes 4-5 servings.

Mushroom Soufflé

  1 lb. fresh mushrooms, sliced
½ cup butter, melted
10 slices bread, buttered, cut into 1-inch cubes
½ cup finely chopped onion
½ cup finely chopped celery
½ cup finely chopped green pepper
½ cup mayonnaise
  2 eggs, beaten
1½ cup milk
¾ teaspoon salt
¼ teaspoon pepper
  1 can cream of mushroom soup
  1 cup grated cheddar cheese

Sauté mushrooms. Place half of bread in 2 quart baking dish. Combine mushrooms, onion, celery, green pepper and mayonnaise. Spoon over bread. Top with half of remaining bread. Combine egg, milk, salt, pepper, pour over bread and refrigerate two hours.

Spread soup over and put remaining bread on top. Bake at 300° for 40 minutes. Add cheese and bake 20 minutes longer.

Makes 10 servings.

Peggy Proft
West Allis, Wisconsin

Onion Cauliflower Bake

1 package (10 ounces) frozen cauliflower, thawed
2 packages (10 ounces) frozen onions in cream sauce
¾ cup shredded process sharp American cheese
¼ cup toasted slivered almonds
1 teaspoon snipped parsley
½ cup canned french-fried onions, crumbled

Cut cauliflower into bite size pieces. Make creamed onions according to package instructions (in saucepan, put 1½ cup water, 2 Tablespoons butter and the 2 packages frozen onions). Cover and bring to boil over medium heat. Turn heat down and simmer four minutes; stirring occasionally.

Remove from heat; stir until sauce is smooth. Add cauliflower, shredded cheese, almonds and parsley. Pour into 1½ quart casserole dish.

Bake at 350° uncovered for 35 minutes. Top with crumbled french-fried onions and bake 5 minutes more.

Makes 6-8 servings.

Onion Pie

    3 Tablespoons butter
2½ lb. Bermuda onions
    1 cup sour cream
    4 Tablespoons sherry
    3 eggs
Salt and pepper to taste
Dash nutmeg
Dash thyme
Dash cloves
    1 9" flaky pie crust
    ½ lb. fresh mushrooms

Heat butter in a heavy cream, stir in onion thinly sliced, and cook it, stirring constantly over low heat, until it is almost transparent. Remove the saucepan from the heat and let the onions cool. Stir in sour cream mixed with sherry and eggs well beaten. Add the following: salt, pepper, nutmeg, thyme, cloves. Line a 9" pie plate with flaky pastry. Fill the shell with the onion mixture, top with 4 slices of Canadian bacon and bake the pie in a moderate oven — 350° until the filling is firm and the crust delicately browned. Serve immediately.

Half a pound of fresh mushrooms, sliced, may be substituted for ½ lb. onions before adding the sour cream mixture.

Makes 6 servings.

Peas Continental

2 Tablespoons butter
¼ cup minced onion
¼ teaspoon salt
2 packages (10-ounces each) frozen peas, cooked and drained
2 cans (4-ounces each) sliced mushrooms, drained
Dash of pepper
¼ teaspoon nutmeg
⅛ teaspoon dried marjoram
2 Tablespoons sherry wine

Melt butter in skillet and cook onion until soft. Cook peas as directed on package, drain. Mix the drained peas with cooked onion, add remaining ingredients, stir well. Heat thoroughly.

Makes 6-8 servings.

Potato Pancakes

a delicious compliment to be served with fillet of
walleye dinner

8 medium potatoes
1 cup flour
2 large eggs
Salt and pepper to taste
Cold meat stock

Grate potatoes raw and let them stand for 5 minutes in cold water to cover. Drain the potatoes and squeeze them dry in a towel. Measure the amount of a raw potato pulp, add an equal amount of cold meat stock, 1 cup flour, 2 large eggs, slightly beaten, and salt and pepper to taste. Beat the mixture vigorously to blend it. Add another cup flour in small amounts, beating after each addition until the mixture reaches pancake batter thickness. Heat a griddle and generously grease it with bacon drippings. Spoon 2 tablespoons of the batter into the pan for each cake. Cook the cakes over medium heat until they are golden brown on both sides, turning the cakes only once. Serve with butter, syrup and apple sauce.

Makes 4 servings.

Wild Rice With Snow Peas

1 cup wild rice
2 scallions
1 Tablespoon butter
1 teaspoon salt
2 cups or more chicken broth (canned, if desired)
¼ lb. (1 cup) snow peas
4 large mushrooms
1 four-ounce can water chestnuts, drained
2 Tablespoons peanut or salad oil
½ teaspoon salt
¼ teaspoon freshly ground black pepper
¼ cup toasted almonds

Wash the rice thoroughly, changing the water several times. Cut the green scallion stems diagonally into 2" lengths. Chop the white part of the scallions finely. Melt the butter in a large saucepan. Add the minced white scallion and saute´ until tender. Add the rice, salt and two cups chicken broth. Bring to a boil, stir once and reduce the heat. Cover tightly and cook over low heat until the rice is tender and the liquid is absorbed, about 35 minutes. If necessary, add more broth as the rice cooks.

Meanwhile, remove the ends and strings from the peas. Cut the mushrooms and water chestnuts into thin slices. Heat the oil in a large skillet. Add the scallion stems, peas, mushrooms, water chestnuts and almonds and saute´ only until the mushrooms are tender.

Transfer the cooked rice and vegetable mixture to a casserole. Add salt and pepper to taste and sprinkle with toasted almonds. Mix lightly and keep hot for serving in a very slow oven.

Makes 4 servings.

Stuffed Zucchini

   1 cup ground ham
 ½ cup soft bread crumbs
 ½ teaspoon dry mustard
 ½ teaspoon salt
 ⅛ teaspoon freshly ground black pepper
   2 Tablespoons minced onion
 ½ cup grated cheese
   2 lbs. zucchini
 ¼ cup oil
   1 clove garlic, crushed
1½ teaspoons cornstarch
 ½ cup canned tomato sauce

Preheat oven to 350°. Combine the ham, crumbs, mustard, salt, pepper, onion and cheese. Wash the zucchini thoroughly and cut it into 3" lengths. Scoop out the centers with an apple corer, leaving a shell ¼" thick. Stuff with the ham mixture. Place the zucchini in a baking pan and add the oil and garlic. Cover and bake until the squash are tender, 45-50 minutes. Remove from the pan.

Mix the cornstarch with the tomato sauce and stir into the pan. Cook over low heat until thickened. Skim off the excess fat and spoon the sauce over the zucchini.

Makes 6 servings.

Zucchini And Mushroom Casserole

1 lb. zucchini, trimmed and scrubbed
Pinch of fresh chopped or dried dill
1 clove garlic
Boiling salted water
½ lb. mushrooms, sliced
3 Tablespoons butter
2 Tablespoons flour
1 cup sour cream
Buttered bread crumbs

Cut the zucchini crosswise into 1" slices, add the dill and garlic and boiling salted water to cover and return to a boil. Reduce the heat, cover and simmer gently until the vegetables are tender, do not overcook. Drain, reserving two Tablespoons of the cooking liquid. Discard the garlic.

Saute´ the mushrooms in butter five minutes, stirring occasionally. Stir in the flour and cook 2 minutes longer. Add the sour cream, zucchini and reserved cooking liquid, stirring constantly. Correct the seasonings and heat thoroughly but do not boil. Transfer the mixture to a casserole and top with buttered bread crumbs. Brown quickly under high broiler heat.

Makes 6 servings.

Frittata Italiana
An Italian omelet with ham and cheese

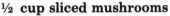

½ cup sliced mushrooms
3 Tablespoons butter
6 eggs, beaten
3 Tablespoons heavy cream
Salt and freshly ground black pepper to taste
Pinch of basil
2 sprigs parsley, chopped
2 Tablespoons grated Parmesan cheese
1 Tablespoon olive oil
½ cup diced cooked ham
Few drops of lemon juice
4 ounces mozzarella cheese, cubed

Preheat oven to 450°. Saute´ the mushrooms lightly in one Tablespoon of the butter and set aside.

Mix the eggs, cream salt, pepper, basil, parsley and one Tablespoon of the Parmesan cheese. Heat the olive oil and one Tablespoon butter in a heavy skillet until the butter turns white. Pour in the egg mixture and cook over very low heat until mixture is still soft on top. Remove from heat.

Sprinkle the top with the mushrooms, ham, remaining Parmesan cheese, lemon juice, mozzarella and remaining butter, melted. Place skillet in oven and bake until the cheese has melted, or about four minutes. Remove to a hot platter and serve immediately.

Makes 4 servings.

Apple And Raisin Stuffing

Great with Goose and Duck

Combine 1 cup chopped onions and their juice with 7 cups soft bread crumbs, 3 cups peeled, cored, and cubed apples, 1 cup parboiled seedless raisins, drained and dried, ½ cup finely chopped parsley leaves, 1½ teaspoons salt, ½ teaspoon each of powdered mace, sage, nutmeg and cloves, 1 garlic clove, finely chopped and 3/4 cup melted butter. Blend thoroughly.

Basic Stuffing Recipes
For Game

1 quart of dried bread crumbs (use day old bread, cold biscuits or leftover corn bread). One quart will stuff one duck.
1 stick of butter
½ cup of chopped onion
½ cup of chopped celery
Salt, pepper and poultry seasoning to taste
2 whole eggs
Hot broth to moisten

Sausage stuffing: add one half pound pork sausage which has been cooked and crumbled into the basic recipe.

Apple stuffing: Use the above basic recipe and add 1¼ cups of chopped apple.

Mushroom Stuffing
for fish

Saute´ 1 small onion, finely chopped, in 4 Tablespoons butter over low heat for 5 minutes. Remove the pan from the heat and mix in 2 - 3 cups soft bread crumbs, ½ pound thinly cut mushrooms, 2 Tablespoons chopped parsley and a few drops of lemon juice. Add about ¼ cup light cream or just enough to moisten the stuffing. Season to taste with salt and pepper. Cool the stuffing before using.

Grandma's Corn Bread

¾ cup of yellow corn meal
¼ cup of flour
2 teaspoons baking powder
½ teaspoon salt
½ teaspoon sugar
1 egg slightly beaten
¾ cup of buttermilk to which ¼ teaspoon of baking soda
   has been added or
¾ cup of sweet milk

Mix all together and pour into heated muffin pans or skillet to which 2 tablespoons of cooking oil or shortening has been added. Bake at 425° for 25 minutes. This may be spiced up by the addition of canned corn, pimentos and jalepano peppers.

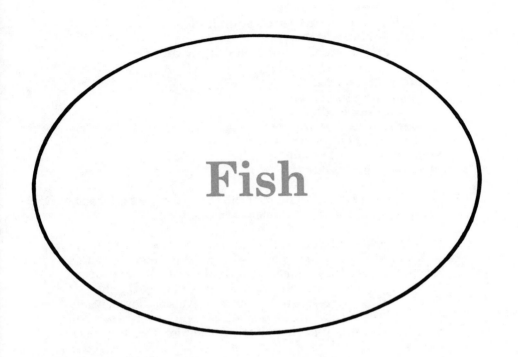

Fish

Door County Walleye Chowder

5 - 6 lb. walleye or 2 three pounders
3 medium onions sliced
3 medium potatoes, peeled and thinly diced
¼ - ½ lb. diced salt pork
1 bay leaf
4 teaspoons salt
1 green pepper diced
4 medium carrots diced
2 teaspoons chopped parsley
½ teaspoon white pepper
2 cups boiling water

Fillet, skin and cut into one-inch chunks. Place the skin, head, bones, and tail into a cheesecloth bag and save.

Sear the pork over medium heat in a dutch oven and turn it until golden brown on all sides. Remove the pork and place on paper toweling to drain. Sauté the onions in the pork fat until clear. Add water and the remaining ingredients and place the cheese-cloth bag of fish parts into the water. Bring this to a low boil and cook until the vegetables are tender; this will require about 20 minutes. Add the fillet chunks to the chowder and cook until they are flaky. Remove the bag of fish scraps and add the tomatoes. Cook the chowder for several more minutes. Garnish with chopped parsley at serving time.

Makes 4 servings.

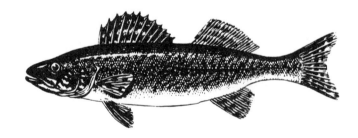

Walleye Pie

½ cup margarine
½ cup celery chopped
1 small onion chopped
4 Tablespoons flour
1½ cups milk
½ cup white wine
¾ cup grated Swiss cheese
1 Walleye fillet cut into bite size pieces (1½ - 2 lb.)
3 eggs
Paprika
1 9" deep dish pie shell, unbaked

Preheat oven to 350 degrees. Melt butter in pan, add chopped celery, onion, and sauté. Blend in flour, salt, pepper. Add milk all at once. Increase heat and cook quickly stirring constantly until mixture thickens. Add wine and cheese, stirring until cheese melts. Now add walleye and allow to simmer. Beat eggs until lemon color and stir into fish mixture. Pour into pie shell and sprinkle with paprika. Bake 45 minutes and let stand 10 minutes before serving.

Makes 4 servings.

Baked Walleye With Vegetable Dressing

3 - 4 lb. walleye fillets (fresh or frozen) soaked a few minutes in lightly salted water

Mix dressing:
1 medium onion, chopped
¼ cup green pepper chopped
¼ cup celery chopped
Sauté in ¼ cup butter till done

2¾ cup dry bread or croutons
½ cup fresh or canned mushrooms chopped
¾ cup shredded carrots
1 Tablespoon snipped parsley (dried can be used)
1½ Tablespoon lemon juice
1 egg beaten
1½ teaspoon salt
¼ teaspoon pepper

Toss lightly all ingredients with sautéed vegetables, adding a little chicken bouillon if too dry. Pat dressing on fish fillet laid on buttered foil in a large pan. Cover with remaining fillet. Sprinkle with a little salt, pepper and paprika; baste with lemon juice and butter. Wrap up and bake. Baste one more time during baking with the lemon juice and butter. Bake in oven 350°. Serve with green salad and baked potatoes.

Makes 6 servings.

Mrs. Frank Decker
Dorchester, Wisconsin

Deep Fried Walleye Fillet
My favorite preparation method

2 lbs. of walleye fillets
4 ounces saltine crackers
3 eggs
¼ cup milk
Salt and pepper to taste
2 fresh lemons (cut into wedges)

Combine eggs and milk and beat until thoroughly mixed. Crush crackers in blender and place in separate dish. Dip fillets in egg mixture then cracker crumbs and deep fry in peanut oil for approximately 3 minutes on each side or until golden brown. Drain on paper towel and place in warming dish. Serve hot with lemon wedges and potato pancakes with applesauce.

Makes 6 servings.

Walleye Italiano

12 medium size fillets
½ cup tomato sauce
2 packages ¾-ounce each garlic-cheese salad dressing mix
2 Tablespoons melted fat
2 Tablespoons chopped parsley
2 Tablespoons grated Parmesan cheese

Clean, wash and dry thawed fish. Combine remaining ingredients except cheese. Brush fillets inside and out with sauce. Place in a well greased baking dish (14 x 9 x 2"). Brush with remaining sauce and sprinkle with cheese. Let stand for 30 minutes. Bake in a moderate oven 350° for 25-30 minutes until fish is fork tender. Turn over control to broil. Place fish about 3 inches from source of heat and broil for 1-2 minutes or until crisp and lightly browned.

Makes 3-4 servings.

Walleye Supreme

8 walleye fillets (2½ lbs.)
1 egg white
¾ cup heavy cream
½ teaspoon salt
2 Tablespoons chopped parsley
3 drops tabasco
1 cup dry white wine

1 small onion, thinly sliced
3 slices lemon
1 bay leaf
3 whole black peppercorns
1 teaspoon salt
¼ teaspoon dried tarragon leaves

Rinse fillets under cold water, pat dry with paper towels. Select six of the best fillets and set aside. Cut the remaining two fillets into 1-inch pieces. Place in blender with egg white, heavy cream, salt, parsley and tabasco. Blend at high speed 1 minute (less if using food processor) until mixture is smooth and light green color. Place the six reserved fillets, dark side up, on a cutting board. Spoon about 2 Tablespoons on each fillet, spread evenly, leaving ½ inch edge all around. Start at narrow end, roll up fillets, fasten with toothpicks. Lightly butter a medium size deep skillet. To keep upright, stand fillets up straight on their more even end, so that they barely touch the side of the pan. Add wine, ½ cup water, onion, lemon, bay leaf, peppercorns, 1 teaspoon salt, and the tarragon. Bring to boil; cover and reduce heat to low. Simmer 10 minutes until center is just firm when tested with a fork. Do not overcook. Lift out with slotted spatula. Drain well (reserving stock). Place on heated platter and keep warm. Make sauce.

Newburg sauce:

3 Tablespoons butter
2 Tablespoons flour
¼ teaspoon salt
⅛ teaspoon paprika

¾ cup light cream
½ cup fish stock
2 egg yolks
2 Tablespoons dry sherry

Melt butter in medium saucepan. Remove from heat, stir in flour, salt and paprika until blended. Cook, stirring several minutes. Gradually stir in cream and ½ cup stock. Cook over medium heat, stirring until mixture thickens and boils; boil 1 minute. In bowl, beat egg yolks. Stir in ⅓ cup hot sauce then stir back into saucepan. Add sherry. Stir over low heat until thick. Spoon some sauce over fish.

Makes 6 servings.

Crispy Walleye With Hot Chili Sauce

6 pan dressed walleye
1 egg beaten
2 Tablespoons milk
1 teaspoon salt
1 teaspoon chili powder
5 - 6 drops liquid hot sauce
½ cup cornmeal
½ cup flour
Fat for frying
Hot chili sauce

Clean, wash and dry fish. Combine egg, milk, salt, chili powder and liquid hot pepper sauce. Mix and combine cornmeal and flour mix. Dip first into egg mixture then roll in cornmeal mix. Place in a single layer in hot fat in large fry pan. Fry at moderate heat about 5 minutes, turn carefully. Fry second side about 5 minutes or until fish are brown and flake easily when tested with a fork. Drain on paper toweling. Serve with chili sauce.

Hot Chili Sauce:
1 cup chopped onion
1 cup chopped green pepper
1 clove garlic finely chopped
1 Tablespoon shortening
2 dashes hot sauce
1 can (8-ounces) tomato sauce
¼ cup ketsup
1 teaspoon chili powder
Salt and pepper to taste

Cook onion, green pepper and garlic in shortening or oil until onion is tender. Add tomato sauce, ketsup, chili powder, salt and pepper and liquid hot pepper sauce. Cover and simmer 15-20 minutes or until flavors are blended. Makes about 1¾ cups sauce.

Makes 6 servings.

Basil Perch

1 lb. perch fillets
1 4-ounce tomato paste
1 small zucchini
1 8-ounce can corn
1 small onion thinly sliced
2 ounce parmesan cheese
Salt and pepper to taste
Basil to taste
1 lemon cut in wedges

Wash and clean fillets. Sauté in lemon butter until flaky.

Before preparing the fish, combine all the vegetables. Mix in the tomato paste and top with Parmesan cheese. Bake at 350° for 20 minutes. Serve hot over fish and top with more Parmesan and freshly squeezed lemon.

Makes 2 servings.

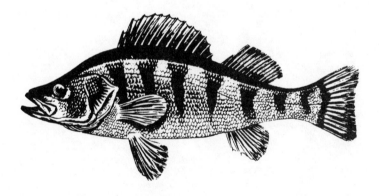

Lake Perch German Potato Pancakes

1 lb. perch fillets
3 eggs beaten
2 Tablespoons flour
2 Tablespoons grated onion
1 Tablespoon chopped parsley
Applesauce
1 teaspoon salt
Dash nutmeg
Hot pepper
2 cups finely grated potatoes

Clean fillets and chop finely. Combine all ingredients except applesauce. Mix thoroughly. Place a well greased griddle or fry pan about 4 inches from heat and heat until fat is hot but not smoking. Drop ⅓ cup fish mixture on griddle and flatten slightly with spatula. Fry 3-4 minutes or until brown. Turn carefully and fry 3-4 minutes longer until brown. Drain on absorbent paper. Keep warm in oven until serving time. Serve with applesauce.

Makes 6 servings.

Chipped Perch

2 lbs. perch fillets
½ cup caesar salad dressing
1 cup crushed potato chips
½ cup shredded sharp cheddar cheese

Dip fillets in salad dressing. Place fillets in a single layer, skin side down, on a baking pan. Combine crushed chips and cheese. Sprinkle over fillets. Bake in an extremely hot oven 500° for 10-15 minutes or until fillets flake with a fork.

Makes 4 servings.

Lake Michigan
Salmon Casserole

2 salmon steaks
2 teaspoons salt
¼ teaspoon pepper
4 Tablespoons butter
2 cups sliced onions
1 cup chopped green pepper
3 stalks celery, chopped
2 Tablespoons cornstarch
2 cups chicken broth made with bouillon
1 cup canned corn kernels
2 Tablespoons soy sauce
1 teaspoon sugar
7 ounces spaghetti noodles, cooked and drained

Cut salmon in 2 inch cubes discarding bones. Dip cubes in mixture of flour, salt and pepper, coating all sides in butter, sauté the salmon, onions, green pepper and celery for 10 minutes. Add to skillet, stirring constantly until it reaches the boiling point, then cook over low heat 5 minutes. Taste for seasoning. Spread spaghetti in buttered casserole and arrange salmon over it. Pour sauce over all and cover the casserole.

Bake in 350° oven with cover on for 30 minutes. Remove cover and cook 5 minutes more.

Makes 2 servings.

Chinook Salmon Loaf

12 ounces salmon
¼ cup milk
¾ cup soft bread crumbs
 2 Tablespoons melted butter
 1 egg
Juice of 1 lemon
 1 Tablespoon scraped onion
½ cup finely minced green pepper
½ teaspoon salt
⅛ teaspoon pepper

Pick over and flake the salmon. Scald the milk and add the bread crumbs and butter. Let stand 5 minutes. Beat until smooth, then combine with the salmon, the egg yolk, seasonings and flavorings. Finally stir in the beaten egg white, transfer to a greased loaf pan and bake in moderate oven 350° about 35 minutes. Unmold and serve hot with tomato sauce or cool them and garnish with the lettuce, tomato, dill weed and mayonnaise.

Makes 6 servings.

Baked Coho With
Sour Cream Stuffing

3 - 4 lbs. dressed coho or other dressed fish
1½ teaspoons salt
Sour cream stuffing
2 Tablespoons melted oil

Thaw frozen fish. Clean, wash and dry fish. Sprinkle inside and salt. Place fish on a well greased bake and serve platter. Stuff fish loosely. Brush fish with fat. Bake in a moderate oven, 350° for 45-60 minutes or until fish flakes easily when tested with a fork. Baste occasionally with fat.

Sour Cream stuffing:
¾ cup chopped celery
½ cup chopped onion
¼ cup melted fat or oil
1 quart toasted bread cubes or herb seasoned croutons
½ cup sour cream
¼ cup diced peeled lemon
2 Tablespoons grated lemon rind
1 teaspoon salt
1 teaspoon paprika

Cook celery and onion in fat until tender. Combine all ingredients and mix thoroughly. Makes approximately 1 quart stuffing.

Makes 6-8 servings.

Broiled Salmon Steaks
With Herb Sauce

6 coho salmon steaks (about 2 lbs.)
¼ cup butter or margarine
¼ cup dry white wine
1 Tablespoon chopped parsley
¼ teaspoon finest herbs blend
1 clove garlic sliced
1 teaspoon salt

Combine butter or margarine, wine, parsley, herbs and garlic; heat slowly until fat is melted. Let stand 15 minutes. Sprinkle steaks with salt. Place fish on well greased broiler pan, brush with sauce. Broil about 3 inches from heat source, 4-6 minutes. Turn carefully, brush with sauce. Broil 4-6 minutes longer or until fish flakes easily when tested with a fork.

Baste steaks with sauce several times while broiling.

Serve with lemon wedges.

Makes 6 servings.

Cold Poached Salmon

1 whole salmon 5-6 lb.

Poach a whole salmon in court bouillon, let it cook in the liquid and chill it. Drain the salmon and remove the skin from one side. Carefully turn the salmon onto a serving platter lined with lettuce leaves, skin side uppermost and remove the skin. The skin on the head and tail should be left intact.

Decorate the salmon with thinly sliced mushrooms that have been marinated in lemon juice and top each slice with a little hard cooked egg yolk. Garnish with sliced mushrooms and deviled eggs.

Makes 8 servings.

Planked Salmon Loaf

     2 cups fresh boiled salmon
    ½ cup soft bread crumbs
     2 eggs
    ¼ cup light cream
     4 Tablespoons butter melted
     1 Tablespoon lemon juice
     1 Tablespoon minced parsley
     1 teaspoon scraped onion
    ½ teaspoon salt
Dash of pepper
Buttered crumbs

Pick over and flake the salmon, discarding any bone or skin.
Add all remaining ingredients, except the buttered crumbs and
blend thoroughly. Shape into a loaf in the center of a pan which
has been oiled and heated for 10 minutes in the oven. Bake in a
hot oven 400-425° about 25 minutes, then sprinkle the buttered
crumbs over the loaf and brown either in the oven or under the
broiler about 5 minutes.

Makes 6 servings.

Coho Corn Pie

3 Tablespoons butter
3 Tablespoons flour
½ teaspoon salt
Dash of pepper
2 cups milk
1 lb. salmon boiled
2 Tablespoons minced onion
1 cup grated cheese
1 can fresh corn
½ cup buttered crumbs

Make a white sauce with the butter, flour, seasonings and milk. Pick over and flake the salmon. Place ⅓ in a buttered casserole and add ⅓ of the sauce to which the onion has been added and sprinkle with ⅓ of the cheese. Repeat the layers twice. Spread the corn over all, top with the buttered crumbs. Bake in a moderate hot oven 375° about 20 minutes.

Makes 6 servings.

French Coho Salmon Parmesana

2 lbs. coho fillets
½ cup thick french dressing
2 Tablespoons lemon juice
¼ teaspoon salt
1 can french fried onions
¼ cup grated Parmesan cheese

Cut fish into serving size pieces. Place fish in a shallow baking dish. Combine dressing, lemon juice and salt. Pour sauce over fish and let stand 30 minutes, turning once. Remove fish from sauce and place in a well greased baking dish (12 x 8 x 2"). Crush onion. Add cheese and mix thoroughly. Sprinkle onion mixture over fish. Bake in a moderate oven, 350° for 25-30 minutes or until fish flakes easily when tested with a fork.

Do not overcook.

Makes 4 servings.

Batter Fried - Smelt

Flavor is improved by use of milk in the preparation and cooking.

5-6 inch fish are soaked in milk for ½ hour befor frying. Dip smelt in batter of 2 eggs, 3 Tablespoons rich cream and enough sifted bread crumbs to bind.

Season with salt and pepper before frying in deep fat.

Sesame Smelt

   2 lbs. pan dressed smelt
1½ teaspoon salt
Dash pepper
   1 cup pancake mix
  ½ cup flour
  ¼ cup yellow cornmeal
1¼ cup milk
   1 jar (2⅛ - 2¼ sesame seeds)

Clean and dry fish. Sprinkle inside and out with salt and pepper. Combine pancake mix, and stir only until blended. Stir in sesame seeds. Roll fish in flour and dip in batter. Place in a single layer in a fry basket. Deep fry and place on absorbent paper.

Makes 4 servings.

Rocky Mountain Brook Trout Almondine

   2 lbs. trout whole (approximately four fish)
   2 Tablespoons lemon juice
   2 teaspoons salt
Dash pepper
   2 Tablespoons chopped parsley
½ cup flour
½ cup melted peanut oil
½ cup blanched slivered almonds

Clean and wash whole brook trout. Sprinkle fish with lemon juice, salt and pepper. Roll in flour. Fry in hot fat at moderate heat until brown. Brown both sides. Cooking time is 10-12 minutes depending on thickness of fish. Remove fish to hot platter. Fry almonds until lightly browned. Add parsley. Serve over fish.

Makes 4 servings.

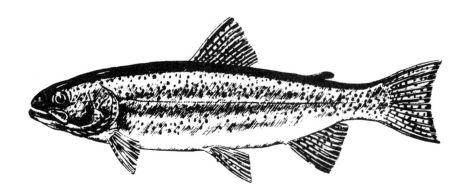

Black Bass In Onion Soup

2 large bass fillets approximately 2 lbs.
Salt and pepper to taste
Liberal dashes of garlic
1 package prepared onion soup mix
1 cup white wine (sauterne)
Paprika

Wash the fillets and dry with paper towel. Place fillets on a large piece of aluminum foil. Season with salt, pepper and garlic powder. Now turn the edges of foil as if to make a bowl. Add the package of onion soup mix, pour in the wine, and sprinkle generously with paprika. Seal tightly and wrap in additional foil. Bake in a 350° oven for about 1½ - 2 hours or until the fish flakes when fork tested.

Makes 4 servings.

Skipper Linguine

6 slices bacon cut into ½ strips
¼ cup sliced green onion
2 cloves garlic minced
6 Tablespoons butter
2 7½-ounce minced clams drained
1 6½-7 ounce blue gill fillet drained and broken into chunks after sautéing or steamed
½ cup sliced ripe olives
¼ cup stripped parsley
⅛ teaspoon pepper
12 ounces linguine
3 ounces grated Parmesan cheese

In skillet cook bacon, drain. Reserve ¼ cup drippings, cook onions, garlic, until tender. Add rest of ingredients. Mix well. Heat and toss hot linguine and add Parmesan to taste.

Makes 4 servings.

Broiled Sturgeon With Lemon Butter

Whip together:
¼ cup soft butter or margarine
1 Tablespoon lemon juice
¼ teaspoon salt
½ Tablespoon chopped parsley

Place prepared sturgeon steaks 1½ inch thick on broiling pan and spread with ½ of the lemon butter. Broil 7 inches from the heat until it is light brown. Turn; spread with the rest of the lemon butter and broil again until brown.

Baked Fillets Of Sturgeon

4 lbs. sturgeon steaks

Butter muffin tins. Line them with thinly sliced fillets, lightly salted allowing them to overlap. Fill them with the following stuffing:

Combine -
  2 cups soft bread crumbs
  ¼ cup chopped onion
  ½ cup melted butter or margarine
  ¼ cup chopped celery
  ¼ teaspoon poultry seasoning
Salt and pepper to taste

Close fillets over top of the stuffing and put a slice of butter or margarine on the top. Place the tins in a pan of hot water and bake in a 370° oven for ¾ hour to 1 hour. Unmold the fillets on a platter.

Makes 8-10 servings.

Northern Pike In
Horseradish Sauce

1½ lbs. northern pike cut into steaks
  1 cup sour cream
  3 Tablespoons milk
  1 Tablespoon cream style white horseradish
  2 Tablespoons lemon juice
  1 teaspoon capers with juice
  1 teaspoon dry mustard
  2 Tablespoons fresh parsley
Salt and pepper to taste
  3 Tablespoons butter

Prepare the sauce by combining the sour cream, milk, horseradish, lemon juice, capers, dry mustard and parsley.

Sprinkle the pike with salt and pepper. Melt the butter in a baking dish and turn the fish over in the butter to coat both sides. Pour the sauce over the fish. Bake, uncovered at 350° for 25 minutes or until fish flakes easily. Garnish with additional chopped parsley and thinly sliced lemon.

Makes 4 servings.

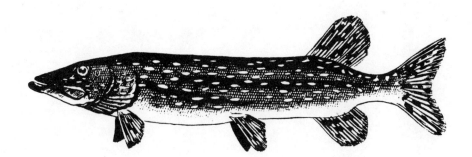

Sweet And Sour Carp

1 cup vinegar
1½ cup water
1 onion sliced
1 lemon sliced
12 raisins
6 whole cloves
Bay leaf
2 lbs. carp fillets
2 Tablespoons brown sugar

Place the first seven ingredients in a sauce pan and bring to a boil. Add the salted fillets, cut into strips crosswise. Reduce the heat and simmer until the fish is done. Remove the fish and add the sugar to the liquid. When it boils, pour it over the fish. Chill and serve cold. Fish will keep for 2-3 weeks in a cold place.

Makes 4-6 servings.

Southern Fried Catfish

6 pan dressed catfish
2 teaspoons salt
¼ teaspoon pepper
2 eggs
2 Tablespoons milk
2 cups cornmeal

Thaw frozen fish. Sprinkle both sides with salt and pepper. Beat eggs slightly and blend in milk. Dip fish in the eggs and roll in cornmeal. Place fish in a heavy fry pan which contains ⅛ inch of melted fat, hot but not smoking. Fry at moderate heat. When fish is brown on one side, turn carefully and brown the other side. Cooking time is about 10 minutes, depending on the thickness of the fish. Drain on absorbent paper. Serve immediately.

Makes 6-8 servings.

Spring Run Creamed White Bass With Ham

2 whole white bass 1½ to 2 lbs. each
1 cup diced ham
1 cup water
1 teaspoon salt
1 teaspoon lemon juice
1 can condensed mushroom soup
1 can sweet milk
½ teaspoon pimento chopped

Place fish in a pot with water, salt and lemon juice. Cover and bring to a boil. Simmer for about 10 minutes, cook and break into small chunks.

Combine condensed mushroom soup and milk in a saucepan and heat slowly. When mixture is about to bubble, add ham, fish and pimento and stir gently until hot. Add a dash of cooking sherry to flavor and spoon mixture over toast.

Makes 4-6 servings.

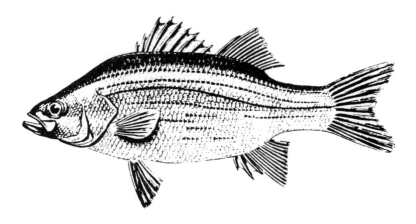

Nagawica Deviled Crappie

(Bluegill)

    4 cups crappie or bluegill
      (drop fillets into boiling water — remove and drain)
    1 cup milk
    ¼ lb. butter
 1½ Tablespoon grated onion
Dash pepper
    3 Tablespoons Worcestershire sauce
    1 green pepper
    4 thick slices white bread (crust removed)
    3 Tablespoons chopped parsley
    ¾ teaspoon salt
Dash tabasco sauce
    1 teaspoon dry mustard
    1 pimento finely cut

Cook everything but the fish for 10 minutes, stirring. Then add the fish and cook five minutes. Put in a fillet casserole. Sprinkle crumbled corn flakes lightly over the top. Then brown in a hot oven 350° 10-15 minutes.

Makes 6 servings.

Brush Crappie Soufflé

1 cup of milk or white wine
3 Tablespoons butter
1 slice white bread
1 teaspoon ready made mustard
Paprika
¼ teaspoon salt
¼ teaspoon nutmeg
1 cup cooked fillets flaked
5 egg yolks
5 egg whites
Parmesan cheese

Heat the cup of milk or wine and 3 Tablespoons of butter until the butter is melted. Pour into a blender, add 1 slice of white bread with the crust — all in pieces — ½ teaspoon ready made mustard, ¼ teaspoon salt and ¼ teaspoon nutmeg. Cover and blend for 5 seconds, then add 1 cup of finely flaked cooked fish and blend for 10 seconds.

Put in the 5 egg yolks and blend 15 seconds more. Beat the 5 egg whites until stiff but not dry and fold them in carefully with a rubber spatula. Butter a souffle´ dish or oven proof individual onion soup dish.

Fill to within ½ inch of the top, sprinkle with Parmesan cheese and a little paprika, set on cooking sheet and bake in moderate preheated 375° oven for 15-20 minutes until puffed and brown. Serve immediately.

Makes 4 servings.

Boiled Crawdads

Wash the crawdads in clean water. Some people soak them for 24 hours in fresh water. Throw out any which are dead before cooking. Bring a large pot of water to a boil with a few peppercorns and bay leaf. Drop the crawdads in and boil 6-10 minutes. They will turn a bright red.

When the crawdads are cool, clean them by twisting off the head and discard it. The claws and tail contain a delicious meat. Shell both.

Dip the tails and claws in lemon butter to appreciate the taste.

Brook Trout Meuniere

6 brook trout
Milk
⅓ cup flour
½ teaspoon salt
Pepper
Peanut oil
⅔ cup butter
Lemon slices
Chopped parsley

Clean the trout, remove the fins but leave the heads and tails on. Dip in milk and drain well.

Mix flour, salt and pepper. Roll fish in mixture.

Heat enough peanut oil in a skillet to cover the bottom to a depth of about ¼ inch. When hot, add trout and brown well on both sides. When cooked, remove to a hot serving platter.

Pour off the fat from the skillet and wipe well with paper towels. Add the butter and cook until it is hazelnut brown. Pour the butter over the trout. Garnish with lemon and parsley.

Makes 6 servings.

Crab Louis

1 cup mayonnaise
⅓ cup French dressing
¼ cup chili sauce
2 Tablespoons minced chives
2 Tablespoons minced green olives
1 teaspoon horseradish
1 teaspoon Worcesterhire sauce
Salt and fresh ground black pepper
Chilled lettuce, torn into bite sized pieces
3 cups cooked crabmeat, flakes
4 hard cooked eggs, quartered
Quartered tomatoes
Capers

Combine the mayonnaise, French dressing, chili sauce, chives, olives and seasonings. Chill. Arrange the lettuce in a shallow, chilled salad bowl and mound the crabmeat on top. Spoon the dressing on top and garnish with hard cooked eggs, tomato quarters and capers.

Makes 4 servings.

Baked Lake Erie Walleye

1 3 to 4 pound (dressed weight) walleye
4 strips bacon
1 onion, medium size, sliced
1 lemon, sliced thin
1 medium size can, plum tomatoes, peeled
1 garlic clove, minced or crushed
Salt and pepper
2 Tablespoons of water
1 Tablespoon butter
Dash of cayenne pepper

Rub fish with salt and pepper and lay in a roaster on bacon strips. Add the water, cover tight and steam for 10 minutes in a preheated 400° oven.

Sauté garlic, onion and tomatoes in the butter, add cayenne pepper and tomato juice. Let come to a boil and pour over the fish. Cover the fish with lemon slices and cook uncovered, 45 minutes in a 325° oven.

This works best with whole fish. It can be used with fillets but they tend to come out on the dry side.

Marilyn Millott
Sandusky, Ohio

Pickled Northern Pike

3 or 4 cups Northern Pike
8 cups vinegar
⅝ cups salt
3 cups sugar
½ box pickling spices
1 whole large onion, sliced

Skin and fillet fish, then cut it into bite size pieces, (lady-like sizes) 3 or 4 cups of da stuff. Mix vinegar and salt. Pour over fishes, and let stand in refrigerator one week....drain fishes, soak 1 hour in cold naked water. Now mix 4 cups vinegar mitt 3 cups sugar and ½ box pickling spices. Bring to boil....then cool.

Put layers of fishes and onions in a gallon jar, pour cooled brine over dis mess. Let stand in refrigerator three weeks. Eat em' up.

In rememberance of,
Ray Chmielecki
Black River Falls, Wisconsin

Bruce's Smoked Salmon

8 - 10 lbs. salmon (cut up into steaks)
Salt (uniodized)

Cut fish into fillets or steaks (skin on). Soak 8-10 hours in uniodized salt (strong enough to float an egg). Wash, bake for 30-40 minutes in oven in a pan with salt, skin side down. Smoke 2 - 3 hours with favorite wood chips. Cool and eat.

Bruce Kirchoff
Waukesha, Wisconsin

Upland Game

Ruffed Grouse (Partridge)

The rich dark meat of the grouse needs brief cooking to bring it to the perfect state of juicy doneness, but it should be well larded in the roasting pan to make up for the natural leanness of its flesh. All the methods of preparation suggested for partridge and quail are equally good for grouse.

Grouse can be eaten within twenty hours of killing, or it can be hung for a brief period.

Ruffed Grouse Cacciatore

    2 2-lb. grouse blue or ruffed
  ¼ cup olive or salad oil
    2 medium onions chopped
    2 green peppers chopped
    1 red pepper minced
    2 cloves garlic minced
    1 clove garlic minced
    3 tomatoes peeled and chopped
1½ cups tomato puree
    2 Tablespoons sour white wine
1½ teaspoons salt
  ⅛ teaspoon pepper
  ⅛ teaspoon allspice

Cut grouse into serving portions and brown in hot oil. Add onions, peppers and garlic and brown lightly. Add remaining ingredients and simmer ½ hour or until bird is tender. Pour sauce over grouse and serve.

Makes 4 servings.

Breast Of Partridge
En Casserole Connoisseur

3 partridges weighing 2 to 2¼ lbs.
⅓ cup butter
1 teaspoon paprika
6 thin slices of Virginia ham
Salt and pepper
Bouquet garni
2 Tablespoons grated orange rind
Marjoram (pinch)
3 Tablespoons red currant jelly
3 Tablespoons rum
1 teaspoon tarragon vinegar

Rub with rum a shallow earthenware casserole large enough to accommodate the breasts of three partridges and in it heat the butter. Stir in paprika, mixing well. Remove the casserole from the heat and add ham, trimmed to fit the breasts. Season the breasts to taste with salt and pepper and a few grains of nutmeg and crushed juniper berries and set them on the ham slice. Add a bouquet garni and sprinkle with 2 Tablespoons grated orange rind and a pinch of marjoram.

In a bowl, combine thoroughly, chicken stock, red currant jelly, rum and tarragon vinegar. Taste for seasoning and pour the liquid over the breasts. Bake the casserole, covered in a moderate oven - 350° for about 30 minutes. Baste the breasts quickly with the cooking liquid, cover the casserole and cook them for 20 minutes longer. Discard the bouquet garni and serve with hot buttered toast.

Makes 4 servings.

Perdix En Casserole
(Partridge in casserole)

Partridge shot in the United States is not a partridge at all, but ruffed grouse. Grouse, partridge, quail all should hang for at least four days to allow its delicate, fragile flavor to develop.

6 plump grouse	**1 cut garlic clove**
½ cup brandy	**Freshly ground nutmeg**
Juice from 1 lemon	**Sheet of larding pork**
Salt and pepper to taste	**(bacon)**
Pinch powdered thyme	**6 Tablespoons butter**
Livers from bird	**2 cups chicken stock**
12 chicken livers	**12 mushroom caps**
6 hard cooked eggs	**3 dozen small green olives**

Clean, pluck and singe 6 plump partridges that have hung for 4 days.
Rub them inside and out with mixed brandy and lemon juice lightly seasoned with salt and powdered thyme to taste. Set them aside.

Skin the 6 partridge livers and 12 chicken livers and put them through the finest blade of a food chopper with 6 hard cooked eggs. Put the mixture in a bowl rubbed with a cut garlic clove, season highly with salt, pepper and freshly ground nutmeg and moisten with ¼ cup brandy. Blend the mixture thoroughly, divide it into six portions, and fill the cavities of the birds. In a flameproof casserole heat 6 generous Tablespoons butter with ¾ cup small cubes of raw lean ham and 1 large bay leaf to the smoking point. Cook the birds in the fat over medium heat, turning them frequently. When they are nicely browned, add 4 whole garlic cloves, parboiled in a little water for about 2 minutes and drained. Cover the casserole and set it in a hot oven 400° for 30 minutes.

Reduce 2 cups chicken stock by half over high heat and add it to the partridge with 12 small mushroom caps, sautéed in butter and well drained, 3 dozen small green olives and 1 Tablespoon lemon juice. Cover the casserole and cook the mixture for 10 minutes longer. Thicken the sauce, if desired, with 3 teaspoons potato starch mixed with 3 Tablespoons cold water. Serve in the casserole, with a glass of red currant jelly mixed with 1 teaspoon drained horseradish, bread sauce and potato chips.

Makes 8 servings.

Iola Ridge Partridge Casserole

   2 partridge breasts and legs
   2 onions sliced
   1 carrot sliced
   1 celery sliced
   1 cup cream of mushroom soup
   1 can evaporated milk
  12 ounces fresh mushrooms sliced
   1 bay leaf
   1 cup dry wild rice, or brown rice

Simmer partridge with onion, carrot, celery and bay leaf for 20 minutes until tender. Cool. Save stock, skim when cool and save for cooking rice.

Bone the meat. Mix mushrooms, soup, evaporated milk, 1 teaspoon salt and ¼ teaspoon pepper and fold pieces of meat in. Place in buttered casserole dish. Bake at 350° for 1½ hours. Serve over rice.

Makes 4 servings.

New Method Perdreaux Aux Choux
(Partridge with cabbage)

6 young partridge
½ cup fiment
½ cup butter
1 Tablespoon flour
Meat stock
¼ lb. diced salt pork
6 sprigs parsley
1 large bay leaf
3 small new cabbages
1 lb. lean fresh pork, sliced
Salt and pepper
Pork sausages

Clean, singe and truss the partridges. Brown delicately in the combined fimet and butter, turning the bird so as to brown on all sides and sprinkling with the flour while cooking. Now add three cups of stock with the diced pork and with the parsley and bay leaf tied together. Simmer 15 minutes. Meanwhile, panboil the cabbage, first removing the heavy ribs. After cooking five minutes, lift out with a perforated skimmer and add to the partridges with the fresh pork slices and more meat stock, using enough to cover the bird. Season with salt and pepper, cover tightly and bake in a moderate oven 350° about half an hour (longer if the birds are old).

To serve, place on a nest of cabbage leaves garnished with pork sausages sautéed in butter.

Makes 4 servings.

Pheasant

Pheasant is generally hung for four days to a week, to bring out the aromatic rich flavor, which is reminiscent of venison and of chicken, and better than both.

Pheasant is lean and should be covered with fat for cooking.

Bavarian Pheasant
With Sauerkraut

4 pheasant breasts deboned
8 medium red potatoes
4 carrots peeled and cut into juliene strips
½ cup butter
½ lb. bacon strips
1 teaspoon caraway seeds
½ teaspoon ground pepper
¼ cup white wine
27 ounce can sauerkraut (drained)

Parboil the potatoes and carrots for about 10 minutes. Immediately drain and set aside.

Brown the pheasant breasts in butter until they are golden brown. Remove the pheasant from the skillet. In the same skillet, fry 2 strips of the bacon to render fat but remove the bacon before it is crisp. Roll the carrots and potatoes in some of the pan drippings for flavor. Set aside again.

In a large mixing bowl, combine the sauerkraut, caraway seeds, pepper, remaining pan drippings and wine. Tear the 2 strips of cooked bacon into small pieces. Add to the mixture and combine thoroughly.

Place half of the sauerkraut mixture in the bottom of a large casserole and top with the pheasant halves. Surround the pheasant with the remaining sauerkraut. Place the potatoes and carrots around the pheasant.

Cover each bird half with 1 strip of bacon. Cover the casserole. Bake at 350° for 45 minutes, occasionally basting the birds and vegetables with the pan drippings. Uncover and bake for another 30 minutes. Continue to baste. The bacon imparts a rich flavor to all the ingredients.

Makes 4 servings.

Pheasant In Sour Cream

1 2½-lb. pheasant cleaned and cut into serving pieces
Salt and pepper to taste
1 cup sour cream
2 sprigs parsley chopped
½ small chopped onion
4 Tablespoons flour
2 pinches tarragon
½ cup white wine
Paprika

Dredge the pheasant in flour. Melt the butter in a large skillet, then sauté the pheasant with onions, wine and butter seasoned with salt and pepper. Remove pheasant and place in open roasting pan. Mix the onions with the sour cream and spread evenly over the pheasant. Generously sprinkle paprika over mixture. Bake at 350° for 1½ hours. Sour cream mixture will help retain the moisture in the bird.

Makes 4 servings.

Apple Cider Pheasant

1 2½-lb. pheasant cleaned, skinned and quartered into
  serving pieces
½ cup butter
Salt and pepper to taste
2 large red ripe delicious apples, peeled, cored and cut
  into large chunks
1 Tablespoon cinnamon
1 cup apple cider

Brown pheasant pieces in butter on all sides in a large frying skillet for about 6 minutes. Remove from skillet and place in dutch oven and add the apples, cinnamon and apple cider. Cover and simmer at 325° for about 1¼ or until the pheasant is tender.

Makes 4 servings.

Pheasant Au Vin

2 whole birds
1 quart port wine
6 chole cloves
2 cups flour
1 bay leaf
1 large onion thinly sliced
Salt and pepper to taste
¼ lb. butter

After birds have been thoroughly cleaned and singed, cut into pieces as you would a chicken. Combine port wine, cloves, onions, bay leaf and sage. Soak pieces in this wine mixture for 2-3 days storing in refrigerator.

Drain the birds, reserving the liquid. Wipe dry and dip in flour to which has been added salt and pepper. Brown on both sides in butter. Turn the birds and liquid and place into a casserole dish. Cover for baking in slow oven 300° for 1½ hours or until tender.

Makes 4 servings.

Pheasant Tarragon

1 lb. wild rice
2 2½-lb. pheasants quartered
2 medium Spanish onions
1½ lb. whole mushrooms
2 cups white wine (one for drinking one for cooking)
1 lemon
2 11-ounce cans cream of chicken soup
½ lb. butter
3 dashes tarragon

Clean and slice large mushrooms combine with chopped onions sautéed in butter at high heat until brown, add wine, cook for an additional 2 minutes until ½ done. Put aside and keep warm.

At the same time, bake pheasant for 1 hour at 325°. While the pheasant is baking, in separate sauce pan heat the cream of chicken soup, a squeeze of lemon and tarragon. Now combine all ingredients and ladle over pheasant and continue to cook for an additional 45 minutes or until fork tender. Baste the pheasant often with sauce.

Serve hot over rice.

Makes 4 servings.

Baked Pheasant And Rice

2 pheasants in serving pieces
1½ ounce envelope dehydrated onion soup mix
14 ounce fresh mushrooms
¾ cups long grain rice uncooked
¾ cup milk
1 10-ounce can condensed cream of mushroom soup

Blend mushroom soup and milk. Combine this with rice, mushrooms and juice and onion soup. Mix and pour into a 13 x 9 x 2" baking dish. Arrange pheasant on top. Brush with melted butter, sprinkle with paprika and bake uncovered in oven preheated to 325° for 1½ hours.

Makes 6-8 servings.

Pheasant Supreme

4 pheasant breasts, deboned
1 cup wild rice
1 cup long grain rice
1 cup sautéed mushrooms

Combine the cooked rice and the sautéed mushrooms. Divide equally and stuff each breast with ¼ of the mixture. Wrap and place in a 13 x 9" baking dish. Season with salt and pepper.

Sauce:
1 can cream of mushroom soup
1 small carton of sour cream
½ cup cooking sherry

Pour the sauce over the breasts. Top with ½ cup of toasted almonds. Sprinkle with paprika. Bake at 350° for 1¼ hours.

Makes 4 servings.

LaVerne Backes
Burlington, Wisconsin

Woodcock With Wine
And Grapes

10 woodcock or doves
    (Cornish game hens)
3 - 4 strips of bacon
Flour
Salt and pepper
 1 cup chicken consommé
 1 cup sauterne wine
 1 stalk celery
 3 carrots thinly sliced
 ½ cups sliced mushrooms sautéed
 2 cups seedless grapes
 ½ cup orange juice

Fry the bacon until it is half cooked, then remove the bacon and
save the drippings. Dredge the woodcock in flour seasoned with
salt and pepper. Sauté the birds in the bacon drippings. Next
arrange the woodcock in a baking dish and place a small piece of
bacon across each breast. Add the consommé, wine, celery stalk
and carrots. Cover and bake at 325° for 20 minutes. Then add
the grapes and mushrooms. Cover and cook for another 15
minutes. Add the orange juice and cover once again for the final
15 minutes of cooking. Remove and discard the celery.

Makes 3-4 servings.

Turkey And Broccoli Almondine

2 cups medium noodles
1 package (10 ounce) frozen broccoli, cooked
2 Tablespoons butter
2 Tablespoons flour
1 cup evaporated milk
1 cup turkey or chicken broth
1 cup diced Cheddar cheese
½ teaspoon monosodium glutamate (MSG)
1 teaspoon Worcestershire sauce
¼ teaspoon pepper
2 cups diced cooked turkey
Salt
¼ cup toasted slivered almonds

Cook and drain noodles, put in shallow baking dish. Cut broccoli into 1 inch pieces and seserve blossoms. Arrange stems on noodles. Make a sauce with the butter, flour and liquids. Add cheese, MSG, Worcestershire and pepper; stir until cheese is melted. Add turkey and salt to taste; pour over ingredients in dish. Arrange broccoli blossoms on top and sprinkle with almonds. Bake at 350° for about 30 minutes.

Makes 4 servings.

Boiled Turkey, Vegetable And Dumpling Dinner

  1 ready-to-cook turkey about 6 lbs.
  5 cups water
  1 onion cut up
  1 Tablespoon salt
  ½ teaspoon pepper
  ¼ cup flour
  2 packages frozen mixed vegetables
Savory dumpling batter

Wash turkey. Simmer with water and next four ingredients. Simmer for 2½ hours or until very tender. Lift out turkey and remove meat from bones, keep hot. Strain broth, thicken with flour mixed with a little cold water. Add mixed vegetables and bring to a boil. Drop in savory dumpling batter by Table-spoonsful. Simmer, covered for 15 minutes. Put turkey on platter, lift out dumplings and vegetables and arrange around turkey. Pour some of gravy over turkey and serve remainder in bowl.

Savory dumpling batter:
  2 cups sifted all purpose flour
  2 teaspoons baking powder
1½ teaspoons salt
  4 egg yolks
  ⅔ cup milk
  ½ cup chopped parsley
  2 Tablespoons chopped green onion tops

Sift dry ingredients. Beat egg yolks with milk; add to dry ingredients together with the parsley and onion tops. Mix until lightly blended.

Makes 4-6 servings.

Turkey Paprika

- 2 large onions, sliced
- 1 clove garlic, minced
- ¼ cup butter
- 1 can (10½ ounce) tomato puree
- ¼ cup paprika
- Salt and pepper to taste
- 2 cups turkey broth or 2 chicken bouillon cubes dissolved in 2 cups water
- 3 cups cut up leftover turkey
- 1 cup sour cream

Brown onions and garlic slightly in butter. Add remaining ingredients except sour cream. Simmer for about 20 minutes. Just before serving, top with sour cream. Serve with noodles or rice.

Makes 6 servings.

Turkey With Welsh-Rabbit Sauce

3 Tablespoons butter
3 Tablespoons flour
1 teaspoon salt
Dash of cayenne
⅛ teaspoon pepper
1 teaspoon mustard
1 teaspoon Worcestershire sauce
2 cups milk
2 cups sharp Cheddar cheese, shredded
4 - 6 slices cooked turkey
Hot toast

Melt butter, blend in flour and seasonings. Add milk and cook, stirring constantly, until thickened. Add cheese and cook until it is melted. Arrange turkey on broilerproof platter, cover with the sauce. Put under broiler until bubbly. Serve on toast.

Makes 4-6 servings.

Almond-Turkey Bake

1 cup shredded Cheddar cheese
1 Tablespoon flour
1 cup toasted slivered almonds
3 cups cooked, chopped turkey
1½ cup celery slices
1 Tablespoon lemon juice
1 cup mayonnaise
½ teaspoon poultry seasoning
½ teaspoon salt
⅛ teaspoon pepper
Pastry for 2 crust 9" pie

Blend cheese and flour. Combine ½ cup almonds, ¾ cup cheese and remaining ingredients except pastry. Mix well. Fit pastry into a 11¾" x 7½" baking dish; trim to 1 inch beyond edge, flute edge. Fill with turkey mixture. Top with remaining cheese and almonds. Bake at 400° for 30-35 minutes. Garnish with lemon twists and parsley.

Makes 6-8 servings.

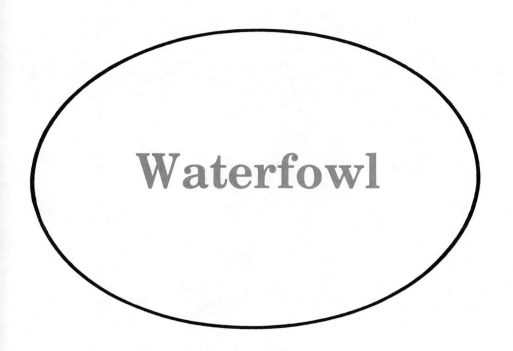

Waterfowl

Waterfowl

Mallard and other wild duck may be hung for at least 24 hours, and preferably for 48 hours before cooking: or the game may be plucked and cleaned and stored in the refrigerator. The oil sacs in the duck's tail should be very carefully removed in the cleaning. The blood of the wild duck retains the best flavor, so the duck should be wiped with a damp cloth, not washed, and it should be served rare.

Some wild ducks eat fish, but the slight fishy taint may be eliminated by putting into the cavity of the otherwise unstuffed bird a whole peeled lemon, or bits of carrots, parsley, and celery, or a small onion and an apple or a strip of bacon.

Mallard Country Club Style

3 ducks dressed cleaned
6 ribs celery washed
Salt and pepper to taste
About 1½ quarts well seasoned bread stuffing
1 cup water
½ cup dry red wine
¼ cup orange marmalade
¼ cup currant jelly
1 thin juice orange diced with rind and all
½ lemon diced rind and all
1 Tablespoon bottle browning and seasoned salt
Dash tarragon
Well seasoned chicken broth about 2 quarts

Preheat oven to 450°. Run cold water quickly through inside of duck to clean it. Sprinkle with salt and pepper and place 2 ribs of celery in each. Roast uncovered, breast side up about 30 minutes until golden brown. Remove from oven, reduce oven temperature to 400°. Pull out celery, let blood and juices drain out. Discard any drippings. Let duck cool slightly, stuff. Place breast side down in roasting pan. Place water, wine, marmalade, jelly, orange, lemon, browning and seasoning salt and tarragon in pan. Add enough chicken broth to just about cover duck. Cover pan loosely with aluminum foil. Bake in a 400° oven until tender (leg will move easily). About 3 hours. Remove duck from pan; keep warm.

Skim fat off gravy. Reduce gravy by boiling. Thicken with flour dissolved in water, if desired. Strain. Serve over duck.

Makes 6 servings.

Before The Show Leftover
Duck Pie

½ package pastry mix
¼ cup fat
1 8-ounce can small whole onions
1 10½-ounce can chicken consomme
⅛ teaspoon pepper
1 teaspoon kitchen bouquet
1 8¾ ounce can diced carrots
2 cups diced duck
½ cup celery diced
¼ cup flour
1 3-ounce can chopped broiled mushrooms
1 teaspoon salt
¼ teaspoon marjoram
1 8½ ounce can potatoes diced
1 8½ ounce can peas

Prepare pastry mix according to directions on package. Roll out
⅛ inch thick and cut 3 inch circles with biscuit cutter. Place on a
baking sheet and prick well with a fork. Bake 375° until lightly
browned, about 10 minutes. Melt fat over moderate heat, add
celery and cook 5 minutes. Stir in flour remove from heat. Drain
onions and mushrooms, reserving broth; add consomme to make
2 cups. Add combined broth to fat mixture and cook, stirring
constantly until gravy thickens and comes to a boil. Add seasonings, onions, mushrooms, drained potatoes, carrots, peas and
cooked duck. Cover and heat thoroughly about 10 minutes.
When ready to serve, pour duck mixture into hot casserole. Top
with circles of pastry and serve at once.

Makes 6 servings.

Hawaiian Honeyed Duck

1 2½ lb. duck cleaned
2 teaspoons salt
1 teaspoon ground ginger
1 teaspoon ground basil
½ teaspoon pepper
¾ cup honey
¼ cup butter
3 Tablespoons orange juice
2 teaspoons lemon juice
1 teaspoon orange peel
⅛ teaspoon dry mustard
1 unpeeled orange cut into ½ inch slices
½ teaspoon cornstarch

Combine the salt, ginger, basil and pepper. Rub half of the mixture inside the duck. Heat together the honey, butter, orange juice, lemon juice, orange peel and mustard, stirring until the butter melts. Rub the inside of the duck with 2-3 Tablespoons of the mixture.

Stuff the duck with orange slices. Pur 4 - 5 more Tablespoons of the honey mixture into the bird. Turn the duck and rub remaining seasoning mixture over the outside of the duck. Place the bird on a large piece of heavy duty aluminum foil. Cover with the remaining honey mixture. Wrap the duck and roast at 325° for 1¾ hours. Unwrap and baste with drippings, then bake for another 20 to 25 minutes or until brown. Place the duck on a hot platter to keep warm.

Combine the cornstarch with a little cold water and add it to the drippings. Stir and heat to boiling. Serve over the duck.

Makes 2 servings.

Braised Duck A La' Orange

5 lb. duck
Salt and pepper
1 cup orange juice
1 cup chicken bouillon
½ cup seedless raisins
Flour
1 small glass currant jelly
Grazed oranges and watercress

Have the duck cut into portions. Wash and pat dry. Brown in a hot dutch oven. Season with salt and pepper, add orange juice, consomme and raisins.

Cover and cook in a slow oven, 300° for two hours without disturbing. Remove the duck to a hot platter, skim off as much fat as possible from the gravy. Add the currant jelly and when melted, thicken the sauce with flour mixed smoothly with a little cold water, using about 1 Tablespoon of flour for each cup of sauce. Pour the sauce over the duck, garnish with glazed oranges and crisp watercress.

Makes 4 servings.

Bayou Barbecued Duck

2 whole mallard ducks - split in half

Barbecue sauce:
- **½ lb. butter**
- **½ cup catsup**
- **1 Tablespoon sugar**
- **1½ Tablespoon lemon juice**
- **1 Tablespoon Worcestershire sauce**

Ground pepper to taste
- **1 teaspoon salt**
- **1 clove pressed garlic**
- **1 chopped small onion**
- **½ teaspoon tabasco sauce**

Simmer covered for five minutes. Make sauce for 4 halves. Now apply liberally over duck piece and grill over the Weber until done to your liking.

Makes 3-4 servings.

Roast Duck Bigarade

Clean a wild duck, rub it with lemon juice, then with salt and pepper, inside and out. Roast in the usual manner, basting frequently either with hot water to which may be added a little butter or with game or meat stock, preferably veal stock. Cook very rare, about 18 - 25 minutes depending on the size of the duck. Serve on a hot platter, garnishing with sections of peeled oranges, slices of lemon and crisp young watercress.

Serve with Bigarade sauce.

Bigarade Sauce

Remove all excess fat from the pan in which the duck was roasted. Sprinkle in ½ teaspoon of flour or cornstarch for two or three minutes. Now add two teaspoons of sugar, caramelized over a low flame and moistened with one Tablespoon of wine vinegar, next the juice of half an orange (lemon juice may be substituted or the two blended). Immediately before serving, add one Tablespoon of grated orange rind and one teaspoon of grated lemon rind.

If a gravy taste is desired, hang the duck in a cold place for a day or two, but never more than three days, this will also help make the bird more tender, expecially of it is old.

Mississippi Mallard Stewed In Red Wine

5 lb. duck
1 teaspoon salt
⅛ teaspoon pepper
2 large onions
3 sprigs fresh parsley — tied with
3 sprigs celery tops and
1 large bay leaf
⅛ teaspoon thyme leaves
¼ cup good brandy
1 pint red wine
1 small carrot thinly sliced
2 slices fat salt pork, chopped
1 Tablespoon olive oil
1 clove garlic minced
½ lb. fresh mushrooms thinly sliced

Cut the duck into portions. Place in a large mixing bowl and add all but the last four ingredients. Blend, and allow them to marinate at least four hours, stirring occasionally. Drain thoroughly, reserving the marinade. Heat the pork and olive oil in a casserole and brown the drained duck pieces on all sides. Add the entire marinade, garlic and mushrooms and let simmer very gently for one hour. Serve from the casserole with rice.

Makes 6 servings.

Mallard Duckling
With Sauce Piquanté

5 lb. duck
Salt and pepper (ground)
1 minced onion
3 Tablespoons fat
2 Tablespoons peanut butter
1 finely chopped pimento
¼ Tablespoon flour
Cayenne
Finely chopped parsley

Cut duck into serving pieces. Simmer in a small amount of water until almost tender. Season with salt and pepper. Sauté with minced onion in fat until brown. To stock, in which duck was cooked, add peanut butter, pimento and flour mixed with water. Cook until thickened, stirring constantly. Season with salt, pepper, cayenne and parsley. Serve duck hot covered with sauce.

Makes 5 servings.

Braised Wild Duck Grand 'Mere

3 ducks
Duck livers
3 - ½ calves sweet bread
Salt and pepper
Ground cloves (pinch)
2 ounces sherry
Pinch powdered mace
14 leeks
3 carrots
3 stalks of celery
1 dozen small onions
1 dozen small mushrooms
1 clove garlic
Bouquet garni
1 cup game stock

Clean, pluck and singe three wild ducks that have hung for two days. Stuff the cavities with the duck livers and ½ calves sweet bread per duck, blanched and cut into cubes. Season the stuffing with salt, pepper and a tiny pinch of powdered mace.

Chop coarsely, the white parts of four leeks and put then in the bottom of an earthenware casserole. Add 1 carrot, sliced, 1 stalk celery, minced, 1 dozen very small white onions, 1 dozen small mushrooms sliced thin, 1 whole clove and bouquet garni. Pour 1 cup game stock. Arrange the ducks on the vegetables in the casserole and pour over them 2 Tablespoons brandy. Bake the casserole, tightly covered, in a hot oven — 400° for 40 minutes.

Serve in the casserole.

Company Wild Duck

2 - 3 lbs. wild duck
1 cup diced onion
1 cup diced celery
2 Tablespoons grated orange rind
½ cup maple syrup
1½ cups Sauterne Wine
Mushrooms — fresh as many as you desire

Cut duck into small pieces and brown in a skillet.

Remove and place in dutch oven or baking dish. Add remaining ingredients to drippings in skillet, mix well. Pour over duck. Bake at 300° approximately two hours or until tender.

Serve with wild rice.

Makes 4 servings.

Irma Biermann
Big Bear Lodge, Winter, Wisconsin

Conard Sauvage A La Presse

3 plump wild ducklings
1 cup warm red wine
6 Tablespoons butter
¼ cup paté de fore gras
⅔ teaspoon celery salt
⅓ teaspoon cayenne
2 lemons juiced
2 Tablespoons cognac
Wild rice
Salt and pepper to taste
1½ ounce brandy

Clean, pluck and singe three plump young ducks that have hung for not more than two days and rub them inside and out with brandy or lemon juice and with mixed salt and pepper. Roast the ducks in a hot oven — 425° for 17 minutes. Put the birds on a heated platter, cover with a silver hood and bring them to the table, where there are a duck press and a hot chafing dish ready. Carve off the six half breasts and cover them in the chafing dish with the blood drained from the ducks during the carving.

Cover the chafing dish and turn up the heat. Put the duck carcasses in a well of the press. Make a smooth sauce from 1 cup slightly warmed red wine, 6 Tablespoons sweet butter melted in hot duck blood, ¼ cup paté de fore gras, ⅔ teaspoon celery salt, ⅓ teaspoon cayenne and the juice of two lemons. Pour it into the press.

Turn the pressure wheel and force the sauce and blood through the press into a heated silver dish. Return the sauce to the press and force it through twice more. Stir in 2 Tablespoons cognac and pour the sauce over the breasts on very hot plates. Serve at once with wild rice.

Makes 6 servings.

Chesapeake Barbecued Duck

Split 2 whole ducks in halves and flatten with side of cleaver. Place on rack in flat bake pan and bake at 375° for 1 hour. Baste every 10 minutes with barbecue sauce. Turn and cook other sides 1 hour. Continue basting.

Sauce:
- ½ lb. butter
- ½ cup catsup
- 1 Tablespoon sugar
- 1½ Tablespoons lemon juice
- 1 Tablespoon Worcestershire sauce

Ground pepper to taste
- 1 teaspoon salt
- 1 clove pressed garlic
- 1 chopped small onion
- ½ teaspoon tabasco sauce

Mix all ingredients and simmer covered for 5 minutes. Makes sauce for 4 halves.

Seven-Minute Mallard

2 mallard breasts (filleted)
2 ounces Worcestershire sauce
3 dashes garlic salt
⅛ cup butter

There is little more meat to a wild duck than the breasts. They should be filleted off the keel bone with a sharp knife. You will wind up with two nice pieces of duck meat that resemble small steaks. The skin can be left on, and the legs saved for making soup, if desired. Or you can remove the skin.

Melt a small amount of butter and add a few squirts of Worcestershire sauce and a small amount of garlic salt. Place fillets on the broiler after salting and peppering both sides. Other seasonings may be added. When the broiler unit is red hot, baste the breasts with the melted butter mixture, slide them directly under the heat and let them sizzle for about four minutes, just like broiling a steak.

Quickly turn over the breasts, baste again and broil for three minutes more, a bit longer if you prefer them done medium. Otherwise they will be on the rare side but crisp and browned appearing.

Avoid letting the meat cool before serving. Use special metal steak insert serving plates that are preheated in the oven. The ducks sizzle when served.

Spit Duckling

4 - 5 lb. frozen duckling, thawed
3 Tablespoons coarse salt
¾ cup red currant jelly
¾ cup orange juice
¼ teaspoon ground ginger
Dash of cayenne pepper
2 Tablespoons cornstarch
1 whole lemon

Squeeze lemon juice over duckling. Sprinkle with salt, inside and out. Refrigerate for 4 hours or longer. Rub off salt with paper towels; do not rinse. Insert spit through duckling tightly. Place spit close to heat source on rotisserie. Cook for 2 hours. Combine jelly, orange juice and ¼ cup lemon juice in saucepan. Warm over medium heat, stirring until well blended. Stir in ginger and cayenne pepper. Blend cornstarch with 2 Table-spoons water; stir into jelly mixture. Bring to a boil. Boil for 4 minutes. Brush duckling with glaze. Cook for 15 minutes longer, brushing with glaze frequently.

Makes 2-4 servings.

Roast Goose And
Stewed Apples

    1 goose
Salt
    4 cups water
    6 peppercorn
¼ lb. butter
½ onion sliced
    2 Tablespoons flour
Stewed apples

Remove wings, neck and feet. Cover with cold water and soak for minutes. Drain and pat dry. Rub with salt inside and out.

Put the bird in a roaster and add water, onion, peppercorn. Roast in moderate oven 325°. After the water has boiled down, baste the bird with the batter that has been browned. Allow about 25 minutes per pound. If the goose appears to be an old one, allow an extra 20 minutes to insure complete cooking.

Place the goose on a warmed platter. Put roaster on burner on top of stove, stir in flour, add 2 cups of water and boil for three minutes until smooth and slightly thickened.

Serve the goose and gravy together with the stewed apples.

Stewed Apples

    2 lb. apples peeled and quartered
    2 Tablespoons butter
½ cup sugar
    1 Tablespoon lemon juice
½ cup water
¼ cup white wine
    1 small piece lemon peel

Stew together until apples are tender and almost transparent. Serve hot.

Makes 6 servings.

Irish Goose

Clean and dry the goose, rub inside and out with salt and pepper mixed at the ratio of 1 teaspoon salt to ¼ teaspoon pepper.

  8 lb. goose
10 medium potatoes, boiled and diced
  1 cup chopped onions
  ¼ teaspoon pepper
  ½ lb. ground salt pork
  1 teaspoon poultry seasoning
  1 Tablespoon fat
  ½ cup chopped celery
  4 slices bread — crumbled
  2 eggs beaten
  1 teasoon salt

Reserve potato water for basting. Put fat in skillet and partially cook onions and celery, but do not brown. Combine all the ingredients into a stuffing mixture, stuff goose and roast in a moderate oven 3-4 hours basting from time to time with potato water.

Makes 6 servings.

Roast Goose With
Baked Apples

8 lb. goose
2 quarts bread crumbs
2 onions chopped
2 Tablespoons fat
1 Tablespoon sage
2 teaspoons salt — dash pepper
6 - 8 apples
¼ cup brown sugar
3 cooked mashed sweet potatoes

Cook the giblets (gizzard, heart and liver) until tender, chop and mix with bread crumbs, onion, fat, sage, salt and pepper. Clean and wash goose thoroughly, but do not stuff. Prick into skin through fat layer around legs and wings. Heat in moderate oven 375° for 15 minutes. Cool to room temperature and repeat two more times. Drain off fat. Rub inside of goose with salt, stuff and truss.

Place in roaster and roast uncovered in slow oven — 325° until tender about 25 minutes per pound. Wash and core apples sprinkle with brown sugar. Stuff with seasoned sweet potatoes and place in pan with goose 1 hour before goose is done.

Serve hot with goose.

Makes 6 servings.

Goose Salad Supreme

½ lb. leftover cooked goose
8 ounce chunk pineapple
1 ounce sliced almonds
½ teaspoon caraway seed
¼ cup mayonnaise
½ cup diced celery
½ tomato

Dice goose and pineapple to bite size, then combine with mayonnaise, celery, salt and pepper to taste. Serve on bed of chilled lettuce, garnished with wedge of tomato. Sprinkle on almonds.

Makes 2 servings.

Braised Goose Flemish Method

1 old goose
1 cup soft bread crumbs
Salt and black pepper
1 or 2 leaves each of sage, thyme and marjoram
2 Tablespoons butter
½ cup celery, parboiled and chopped fine
1 goose liver
White wine
1 cup chopped ham
Carrots, celery, onions
1 cup chicken stock
1 Tablespoon gin

Combine all ingredients except the liver, wine and the goose itself. Crush the liver with a fork, then add it to the stuffing and blend thoroughly, moistening with white wine to the consistency of any ordinary stuffing. Fill the body cavity of the bird which has been cleaned and singed with the mixture. Skewer or sew the vent and truss.

Place in a braising kettle the raw ham, then the braising vegetables (carrots, celery, onion etc.). Set the stuffed bird over these and pour over it a cup of good chicken or game stock to which the gin has been added. Cover closely and cook in a hot oven — 400° about 1½ hours without disturbing. Lift out the bird, place on a hot platter, brush over with melted fimet (French extract) and keep hot.

Remove any excess fat from the braising kettle. Place over a hot fire and sprinkle in a scant Tablespoon of flour. Bring to a rapid boil, stirring constantly. Add ½ cup of white wine, again bring to boiling point and strain through a fine sieve, pressing a little to extract all liquid from the vegetables. Garnish with apple rings and wild rice.

Makes 6 servings.

Braised Wild Goose Or Turkey

Wild goose and wild turkey differ from their tame cousins by the leanness of their meat. Allowing for this, they may be prepared in the same ways.

1 **wild 8 lb. goose**
2 - 3 **sprigs of parsley**
1 **stalk celery**
1 **bay leaf**
Pinch thyme
1 **quart stock or consommé**

Clean, pluck and singe a wild goose and stuff it if desired. Truss the legs and wings close to the body and cover the bird with slice of fat salt pork. Roast the bird in a hot oven, 400°, until it is well browned. Remove the fat from the roasting pan and add vegetables, 1 bay leaf, a little thyme and a quart stock. Cover the pan and continue cooking, basting often for 2 - 3 hours or until the bird is tender. Strain the gravy and thicken it with 1 Tablespoon of cornstarch mixed with 2 Tablespoons water.

Serve with cranberry sauce or applesauce and wild rice or corn fritters.

Makes 6 servings.

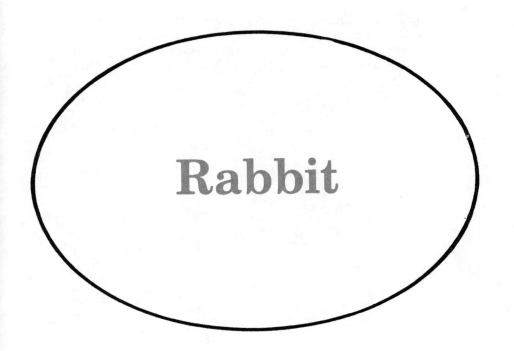

Rabbit

Rabbits

Rabbits and hares have fine textured, lightly gamey meat that somewhat resembles chicken meat. Rabbits also have prodigious talent for propagation, which has been the salvation of this species since it is a favorite with hunters and diners alike.

Hasenpfeffer

This spicy dish is similar to the traditional Sauerbraten

2 2-lb. rabbits cut up

Hasenpfeffer Marinade:
1½ cups vinegar
  1 cup dry red wine
  2 onions sliced
  1 shallot bud, sliced
  2 bay leaves
  6 whole cloves
  ¼ cup flour
  ⅓ cup bacon drippings
  ¾ cup red currant jelly
  1 teaspoon each of salt, pepper and dry mustard
  1 Tablespoon thyme
Pinch of mace

Combine all the ingredients with 1½ cups water in a large bowl. Place the rabbit in the marinade; cover and refrigerate for 24 hours, turning the meat in the marinade once or twice. Remove the rabbit from the marinade and dry the pieces with a paper towel. Strain the marinade; also reserve 1 cup of onions from the marinade. Dredge the rabbit lightly in the flour and reserve the remaining flour. Pour the bacon drippings into a large skillet and brown the rabbit pieces on both sides. Remove the rabbit to an ovenproof casserole. Sauté the onions reserved from the marinade in the bacon drippings. When the onions are golden, remove them with a spoon — draining the grease and add them to the rabbit.

Pour off the bacon drippings remaining in the skillet. Soften the jelly by stirring with a spoon, mix into marinade. Bring to a boil, then reduce the heat. Add enough water to the reserved flour to make a paste. Slowly stir the flour paste into the marinade mixture until the sauce reaches the desired thickness. Pour the sauce over the rabbit. Cover the casserole and place it in a 350° oven for about 1½ hours or until the rabbit is tender.

Serve with buttered noodles.

Makes 4 servings.

Civet Of Rabbit

1 rabbit
4 Tablespoons brandy
1¾ cups oil
Salt and pepper
3 medium sized onions
½ lean pork (fresh)
3 Tablespoons butter
3 Tablespoons flour
Red wine
1 bouquet garni

Place the meat in a large bowl with the brandy, oil, seasonings and one onion cut into thin rings. Allow them to marinate for two hours, stirring frequently, then lift out the meat and pat dry. Dice the pork and brown it in the butter until delicately colored, lift out and set aside.

Brown the two remaining onions, peeled and quartered in the same fat. Sprinkle in the flour and cook until both butter and flour are thoroughly browned and blended. Add the rabbit and sear on all sides. Half cover with red wine, add bouquet garni and garlic, cover and simmer gently for 45 minutes.

Arrange for serving, garnish with the cubes of pork, glazed onions and mushrooms and croutons of bread fried in butter.

Rabbit and Broccoli Casserole

1 large rabbit about 2 lbs.
1 package frozen broccoli spears
1 can cream of chicken soup
1 cup grated Cheddar cheese
Salt and pepper to taste

Simmer rabbit in a salted kettle of water with onion and carrots and celery, chopped, for 1 - 1½ hours or until meat falls from the bones. Let rabbit cool, then bone it. Place rabbit pieces in the bottom of a buttered casserole dish. Spread the thawed, drained spears of broccoli over the top. Pour the cream of chicken soup over the whole dish. Salt and pepper to taste. Bake at 325° for 1 hour. Take out and sprinkle cheese on top. Return to the oven until cheese is melted.

Lemon Rabbit

1 2½-lb. young rabbit
2 teaspoons salt
¼ teaspoon pepper
6 Tablespoons shortening
1 cup chicken broth
3 Tablespoons lemon juice
6 Tablespoons orange juice
1 small onion chopped
Dash ginger
1 cup sliced mushrooms

Dredge rabbit pieces with flour, seasoned with 1 teaspoon salt and ⅛ teaspoon pepper. Sauté until well browned in the shortening. Drain off excess fat. Add chicken broth, lemon and orange slices and juices and onions.

Season with 1 teaspoon salt, ⅛ teaspoon pepper and ginger. Cover and simmer over low heat until tender, about 1 hour. Add mushrooms for the last 15 minutes of cooking. Thicken juices with a little of the seasoned flour mixed with a little water.

Hunters Rabbit

1 rabbit
1 cup olive oil
1 clove garlic
1 cup all purpose flour
2 Tablespoons dry mustard
1 teaspoon curry powder
1 teaspoon powdered thyme
2 teaspoons salt
⅜ teaspoon pepper
1 cup light cream

Cut rabbit into serving pieces brushed with oil, and refrigerate overnight. Next day, rub pieces with cut clove of garlic. Combine flour, salt, pepper and spices in a clean paper bag. Shake pieces of rabbit in bag until well coated. Fry to a golden brown in oil, turning until crisp. Reduce heat to simmer and pour cream over rabbit. Cover, simmer for 1 hour or until tender. Serve on a hot platter with cream sauce.

Makes 2 servings.

Rabbit With Dark Raisin Gravy

1 to 2 rabbits cut into quarters
½ cup vinegar
2 teaspoons salt
1 Tablespoon minced onion flakes or 1 small onion chopped
4 whole cloves
2 bay leaves
½ teaspoon allspice (optional)
½ cup dark raisins
¼ cup brown sugar

Place rabbit pieces in deep pot and cover with cool water. Add ¼ cup of vinegar to water and bring to boil. Let boil for 5 minutes, then throw that water out. Again, cover rabbit with cool water and add ¼ cup vinegar, 2 teaspoons salt, onion, bay leaves, cloves and allspice. Cook until almost tender and then add raisins and brown sugar. Continue cooking rabbit until it is tender and done. Remove rabbit from pot and thicken liquid with a paste of flour and water. Replace rabbit in thickened gravy and heat just before serving.

Smothered Rabbit
Bisquick Style

Saddle and legs from 2 rabbits
 1 cup flour
 ½ cup chopped onion
 ½ cup chopped celery
 2 Tablespoons salt
 1 Tablespoon pepper
 1 teaspoon thyme
 ½ teaspoon oregano
 ½ teaspoon basil
Shortening or cooking oil
Bisquick

Combine flour and all five spices in a heavy paper bag. Shake well. Put rabbit pieces in the bag and shake again. Be sure each piece is coated with seasoned flour. Brown pieces in skillet over medium heat.

When meat is brown, remove from skillet and pour off most of the shortening, leaving about ¼ cup in a skillet. Sprinkle ¼ cup seasoned flour in the skillet and stir with a fork until flour browns.

Add rabbit, celery and onions, cover with cold water and simmer covered for 1 hour until meat is tender.

Make a Bisquick dough using directions on box.

Rabbit Gumbo

2 small rabbits or 1 large rabbit
½ cup oil or shortening
½ cup flour
½ cup chopped onions
½ chopped celery
1 lb. fresh or frozen whole okra
1 teaspoon thyme
1 teaspoon marjoram
2 teaspoons liquid crab boil
¼ teaspoon black pepper
Salt to taste

Cut rabbit into pieces and simmer in a covered pot for 1 hour. Meanwhile, make a roux (gravy) with flour and shortening in an iron skillet. Stir constantly until brown. Add onions and celery and stir until vegetables are soft. Remove from heat and set aside.

When rabbit is through simmering, remove meat from bones, reserving the stock for later use. Combine roux, meat and stock in a heavy aluminum pot (cast iron turns okra black; stainless steel causes gumbo to burn). Add remaining ingredients, and more water if needed.

Cover and cook over low heat, stirring often, for about 1 hour until the okra disintegrates. Pour over rice.

Makes 10-12 servings.

Barbecued Rabbit

2 rabbits, quartered
1 cup salad oil
¼ cup vinegar
¼ cup red wine
1 small onion, minced
1 clove garlic, minced
Juice from ½ lemon
4 Tablespoons Worcestershire
4 Tablespoons A-1 sauce
4 Tablespoons catsup
⅛ teaspoon cayenne pepper
Several drops tabasco
1 teaspoon celery salt
¼ teaspoon black pepper

Combine all sauce ingredients and simmer 20 minutes, stirring frequently. Baste quartered rabbits generously with sauce and grill over charcoal. Turn every 5 minutes and baste heavily each time. Meat should be ready to fall off the bone in 30-40 minutes. Serve with corn on the cob, coleslaw and fresh rolls.

Makes 6-8 servings.

Raccoon Trapper Style

Clean and skin raccoon allowing them to hang in the open air for several hours, then place in refrigerator for at least 24 hours before cooking. Stuff with an ordinary bread stuffing (sage preferred).

Set in a deep pan so that no part will project above the top. Season well with pepper and salt and pour about one inch of beef stock or canned beef bouillon into the pan.

Fill with peeled sweet potatoes and sprinkle a little flour over the whole; cover with a crust the same for a pot pie, omitting the fat as the crust will be removed after baking and will not be served.

Allow to bake slowly for about three hours. Remove crust and serve hot. The crust will absorb most of the fat from the coon.

Squirrel Pot Pie

    1 squirrel
    3 cups water
    1 diced carrot
    ¼ cup diced onion
    1 stalk celery, diced
    1 teaspoon salt
    5 peppercorns
    ⅛ teaspoon pepper
    1 frozen pie shell, cooked
Flour
    2 cups mashed potatoes

Cook meat, carrot, onion, celery, salt, peppercorns and pepper in water until tender. Let cool, debone squirrel, and return meat to broth. Add enough water to the meat to make the desired amount of gravy to put in the pie shell. Cover pie with potatoes and place in hot oven for five minutes.

Makes 2-3 servings.

Venison And Big Game

Venison And Big Game

The White Tail Deer, from my experience, are the most difficult big game animals in North America to hunt, and despite their adaptability to an ever-growing society, they are a challenge.

I spent my boyhood hunting the cedar swamp area of Waupaca County and it was not unusual to see two or three bucks and 25 does on opening day.

Despite the water filled, cedar choked jungle these swamp deer resided in, they had the luxury of dining regularly on some of the sweetest corn in all Wisconsin. I truly believe you are what you eat and these deer, no matter what their age, are delicious.

Some venison people attempt to prepare they claim "taste like liver — quite wild tasting."

Well, it stands to reason that when a deer has been chased and shot at through a barrage of hunters, the adrenaline is flowing and he is extremely tense. These conditions will make the meat tough and strong tasting.

If you can get away from the crowd in areas that are remote and tough going, you will probably not only have an opportunity at a larger buck, but also one that will be much more relaxed and will taste better.

Venison, if prepared properly, will taste as good as any milk fed beef. All large game must be hung for periods ranging from three or four days to six weeks or longer before they are ready to eat, much as beef must be hung until it is tender. Wild meats are leaner than domestic meats and need fats for cooking; they are often larded or blanketed with larding pork.

Opening Day Venison Tenderloin

On the day of the hunt, one of the greatest rewards is to be able to further enjoy your trophy by freshly preparing the tenderloin as part of the celebration.

1 whole tenderloin
Worcestershire sauce
Butter
5 slices bacon

As soon as the deer is hung up and cooling, cut out the tenderloin by inserting the blade along the backbone while pulling the meat away with your left hand.

Trim all silver skin and fat from meat. Cut into small steaks. Sauté in butter with sliced onion, Worcestershire sauce. Wrap with bacon and serve with a toothpick. Accompany with wine.

Makes 6 appetizer servings.

Creamed Venison On Biscuits

1 lb. ground venison
1 small onion chopped
1 Tablespoon vegetable oil
3 Tablespoons all purpose flour
2 beef bouillon cubes
1 teaspoon Worcestershire sauce

Sauté meat and onion in oil in a skillet until brown. Drain off excess oil. Add remaining ingredients and simmer for 20 minutes. Serve over biscuits.

Makes 4 servings.

Biscuits
  2 cups sifted all purpose flour
  3 teaspoons baking powder
½ teaspoon salt
  4 Tablespoons vegetable shortening
¾ cup milk

Sift dry ingredients together and cut in shortening. Add milk to make a soft dough. Place on a lightly floured board and knead a few seconds. Roll out ½ inch thick and cut with floured biscuit cutter. Place on a greased baking sheet and bake in a 450° oven for about 12 minutes. Makes 14 2" biscuits.

Makes 6 servings.

Sweet Apple Venison
With Herbs

5 - 6 lb. venison roast
1 Tablespoon cooking oil
2 teaspoons salt
¼ teaspoon pepper
¼ cup flour
1 teaspoon marjoram
1 teaspoon thyme
1 teaspoon rosemary
1 clove garlic crushed
1 cup apple cider
1 cup water

Dry meat well and cut several deep slits in the roast. Sprinkle with salt and pepper. Combine flour, marjoram, thyme, rosemary and garlic and add just enough water to make a thick paste. Cover the roast, pushing some of the paste into the slits. Place the meat in a shallow pan surrounded by the cider and water. Bake uncovered in a 325° oven about one hour. Baste with the pan juices, cover, and roast for about 2 more hours. Baste every 20 minutes or so. Slice thinly.

Will serve 10, or plan on leftovers.

Lumberjack Deer Cutlet

6 thin venison rib cutlets
½ cup olive oil
1 lemon
4 ground peppercorns
1 Tablespoon parsley minced
1 small piece of bay leaf
1 small garlic clove
Salt and pepper to taste
6 Tablespoons marinade
2 Tablespoons sherry
1 small lime or lemon
2 dozen fresh mushrooms

Cut 6 thin slices from the loin of a young deer and sprinkle them with salt and black pepper. Marinate the meat for 1 hour in ½ cup olive oil mixed with the juice of 1 lemon, 4 coarsely ground peppercorns, 1 generous Tablespoon minced parsley, 1 small piece of bay leaf, 1 small garlic clove - crushed and salt to taste. Wipe the cutlets dry and put them in a generously oiled baking dish. Pour over them 6 Tablespoons marinade and 2 Tablespoons sherry. Bake the cutlets in a hot oven - 400° for 20 minutes, basting every 5 minutes. Arrange the cutlets in a ring on a heated platter and squeeze over them the juice of a small lemon. Fill the center with 1 dozen freshly broiled mushrooms.

Serve with cream sauce flavored with 1 teaspoon gin and a dish of currant jelly mixed with equal amounts of drained horseradish.

Makes 2-3 servings.

Venison Steak
Gameskeeper Style

3 lb. venison steak
½ teaspoon ground pepper
½ cup juniper berries (crushed)
¼ cup butter
1 Tablespoon parsley chopped
1 teaspoon chives
1 cup red currant jelly
3 Tablespoons Port wine

Rub 3 lb. steak with mixed pepper and crushed juniper berries to taste. Dip the steak in melted butter and brown it well on both sides on a greased broiler oven — over hot fire. The length of the broiling time will depend on the thickness of the steak, but it should be rare or medium rare. Put the steak on a heated platter and spread it with butter mixed with finely chopped parsley, chives to taste. Mix together 1 cup red currant jelly and 3 Tablespoons Port wine and pour the mixture over the steak. Garnish generously with watercress and serve with shoestring potatoes.

Makes 6 servings.

Cabin Fever Venison Sausage

4 lbs. venison scrap meat from neck, backbone, shank or breast
1 lb. beef fat
2 teaspoons salt
1 teaspoon black pepper
⅛ teaspoon cayenne
2 teaspoons ground sage
½ teaspoon ground allspice

Put venison and beef fat through meat grinder. Mix in seasonings and put through grinder again. With hands, shape meat into 4-ounce patties. The sausage can be prepared any way you like it, or frozen for later use. For best results, freeze patties two to a package.

Scott Darrohn
Rivertown, Wyoming

Pizza Sausage Pie

12 ounces Mozzarella Cheese (sliced)
1 lb. Italian sausage
2 green peppers
1 lb. small perfect mushrooms
8 cups pizza sauce
Pizza dough pre-prepared

Take a 1 lb. or 2 lb. crock bowl with handle and thoroughly grease inside of bowl. Add 2½ oz. of cheese in the bottom of the bowl overlapping the edge. Add the sausage and pizza sauce, then top with julienne strips of green pepper, 3 or 4 mushrooms per bowl and top with pizza dough. Place dough on bowl overlapping about 1 in. all around. Bake at 500° for about 7 min. or until done. To serve, invert bowl on a serving plate and slice away crust from lip of bowl and lift away bowl. The pizza pot pie should be a scrumptious delight engulfed in cheese.

This recipe is being featured in a number of restaurants.

Venison Linguine

1½ lbs. venison stew meat, cubed
1½ Tablespoon cooking oil
1½ cups beer
2 beef bouillon cubes
1 onion sliced
1 Tablespoon horseradish
2 teaspoons steak sauce
3 drops Tabasco sauce
½ teaspoon thyme
½ teaspoon dill weed
¼ teaspoon allspice
Salt and pepper

Brown the venison cubes in the oil in a heavy skillet. Add the rest of the ingredients, correct the seasonings, cover and simmer for 2½ hours. Thicken the liquid with instant flour and serve over a bed of buttered noodles with a sprig of parsley for garnish.

Makes 4 servings.

Poyha

1 lb. ground venison
1 no. 303 can whole kernel corn
1 small onion chopped
1 teaspoon salt
2 eggs
½ cup cornmeal
½ cup water

Measure the cornmeal and place in a small bowl. Add the water and stir to mix. Allow to stand. Brown the venison in fat. When meat is thoroughly cooked, add the corn and onion. Cook 10 minutes. Add the salt, egg and cornmeal. Stir well. Cook another 15 minutes, then put in a greased loaf pan and bake 30-45 minutes at 350°. Serve with cheese sauce or mushroom soup.

Makes 2 servings.

Venison Camp Chili Texas Style

2 lbs. ground venison
1 large onion
2 16-ounce cans chili beans
Dash tabasco
1 chili pepper
½ ounce chili powder
1 cup diced celery
3 16-ounce cans stewed tomatoes
Dash sugar
8 ounce glass of wine (for cooking)

Combine onion, chili beans, tabasco, chili pepper, celery, stewed tomatoes, sugar, simmer for 1 hour in large kettle. Brown venison with ½ onions and drain liquid. Add to the sauce, cook at low heat for an additional hour.

Add the remaining kidney beans and chili powder and cook at low heat for another hour.

NOTE: Chili powder should be added toward the end of the cooking because it is readily destroyed and diluted by heat.

Makes 4-6 hearty servings.

Corned Venison

20 lbs. venison
1 cup brown sugar
2 Tablespoons salt peter
3 cups coarse salt

Dissolve salt peter, brown sugar and salt in 4 cups hot water. Put in large crock (no metal container). Add enough water to cover venison by 2-3 inches. Weight venison down with a plate and clean rock on top. Cure 10-14 days in a cool place. Rinse venison and put in large cooking pot and add the following:

1 Tablespoon thyme
2 Tablespoons salt
1 large onion
1 teaspoon paprika
4 bay leaves
⅓ Tablespoon pepper

Water enough to keep meat covered. Cook at medium heat 3-4 hours until tender. Serve hot or cold. Cut into meal sized servings and freeze.

Makes 25-30 servings.

Venison Stroganoff

2 lbs. round steak (cut into small cubes)
1 cup sour cream
1 bay leaf
Pepper to taste
1 small can mushroom pieces
4 Tablespoons butter
2 teaspoons celery salt
2 Tablespoons Worcestershire sauce

Cut round steak into small cubes. Roll in flour, salt and pepper and brown in hot butter. Add ½ cup water and ½ cup vinegar and simmer until tender. Add water as necessary to keep from burning. When tender, pour off excess liquid. Add sour cream, bay leaf, salt and pepper, mushrooms, butter, celery salt and Worcestershire sauce.

Cover, simmer until everything is heated through. Don't boil. Serve over egg noodles.

Makes 6 servings.

Burgundy Venison Steak Tips

2 lbs. venison steak cut in small cubes
3 Tablespoons oil
2 Tablespoons dry onion soup mix
3 beef bouillon cubes
2 cups water
1 cup burgundy wine
1 cup fresh mushrooms

Brown meat in hot oil. Add remaining ingredients and simmer for about 1 hour. Add mushrooms the last 5 minutes. Serve over fluffy rice.

Makes 4 servings.

Venison Swiss Steak

2½ lbs. venison
½ teaspoon salt
½ cup flour
Dash of pepper
2 Tablespoons butter
½ cup green pepper chopped
½ cup chopped onions
1½ cup water
1 small can tomato paste
1 Tablespoon bead molasses

Trim all fat from venison. Roll meat in salt, pepper and flour. Brown meat in tomato paste, bead molasses, green peppers and onions. Bring to a simmer for about 2 hours, stirring occasionally. Serve piping hot with boiled parsley potatoes.

Makes 6 servings.

Huxley Venison On Toast

  2 lbs. venison (ground)
½ medium onion chopped
½ chopped green pepper
½ teaspoon ground pepper
½ teaspoon salt
½ teaspoon Poupon mustard
  1 ounce catsup
  1 egg
12 slices of white bread

Combine all ingredients: venison, onion, green pepper, pepper, salt, Poupon mustard, catsup, egg and mix thoroughly, in a large bowl. Scoop out mixture with a fork and spread on bread slices. Place on open grate of oven and cook for 15-20 minutes at 400°

Great for afternoon of Sunday football.

Makes 4 servings.

Ground Venison Taco Salad

1 lb. ground venison
1 medium onion
8 ounces taco dorito chips
1 large tomato
8 ounces kidney beans
1 teaspoon ground pepper
4 ounces creamy onion dressing
4 ounces green goddess dressing
1 medium head of lettuce
2 ounces butter

Prepare lettuce in a large salad bowl and toss with tomatoes, kidney beans, dressings, salt, pepper and ½ onion. Set aside. Brown meat with the other ½ onion and butter. Drain. Combine all ingredients and toss again, now mixing crumble taco chips.

Serve garnished with cling peaches.

Makes 4 servings.

Ranger Chops Modenesé

4 venison chops
4 slices of baked ham
2 6-ounces of tomato paste
3 ounces Mozzarella cheese
1 large onion
½ teaspoon basil
½ teaspoon garlic
½ teaspoon oregano
½ teaspoon rosemary
1 lb. fresh mushrooms
¼ cup olive oil

Brown meat in large skillet with olive oil and sliced onions. Remove and place in baking dish. Previous to browning the meat, combine tomato sauce, basil, garlic, oregano, and simmer for 45 minutes.

Ladle sauce over meat, top with slices of ham. Cook at 325° for 45 minutes then add slice of cheese on top. Return to oven for an additional 5 minutes. Serve piping hot.

Goes well with a side dish of buttered vermicelli.

Makes 2 servings.

Burgundy Venison

2 lbs. venison round
1 garlic clove
3 medium onions
4 Tablespoons butter
Salt, pepper, flour
½ teaspoon marjoram
½ teaspoon oregano
½ cup burgundy wine
½ pint sour cream
6 ounces sautéed fresh mushrooms

Cut venison into one inch cubes. Tenderize and set aside. Sauté garlic, onions and butter until soft and brown. Remove onion and garlic from pan. Brown venison slowly in drippings. Return onions and garlic to pan. Add flour and water to thicken gravy. Add salt and pepper. Simmer 1½ hours. Add mushrooms, herbs and wine. Simmer an additional 15 minutes. Add sour cream and serve over wild rice.

Makes 6 servings.

Venison Tomalé Casserole

1 Tablespoon butter
1 lb. ground venison
2 teaspoons salt seasoned
1 teaspoon chili powder
½ teaspoon Worcestershire sauce
1 16-ounce can stewed tomatoes
1½ cups milk
1 egg
¾ cup yellow corn meal
2 cups fresh whole kernel corn
¾ cup sharp Cheddar cheese shredded

Heat oven to 350°. Melt butter in skillet over moderate heat about 250°. Add meat and stir until lightly browned. Add seasoned salt, chili powder, Worcestershire and tomatoes. Beat milk and egg together in a large bowl. Stir in corn meal and corn. Add meat mixture and pour into buttered 2 quart casserole dish. Bake uncovered 1 hour and 10 minutes.

Sprinkle top with cheese, bake 10 minutes more or until cheese is melted and serve.

Makes 6 servings

Melody Hughes
Glendale, Wisconsin

Sour Mash Venison

1 hindquarter venison

Sour mash whiskey marinade:
1 cup whiskey
1 teaspoon celery seeds
6 whole peppercorns
Garlic to taste
1 12-ounce can concentrated orange juice
3 Tablespoons concentrated liquid smoke

Combine the marinade ingredients in a large pan. Put the venison in a pan, spoon marinade on top. Cover and refrigerate for 24-36 hours, occasionally turning the meat in the marinade.

Lightly oil the barbecue grill and place the meat on top of the grill. Baste the venison with marinade at 15 minute intervals. Turn the meat after ½ hour. Barbecue for another 30 minutes.

Venison Stew

1 lb. boneless venison or beef stew meat cut into ½ inch
1½ cups water
1½ teaspoon salt
⅛ teaspoon coarsely ground pepper
½ cup dry red wine
4 medium carrots, cut into thirds
2 medium potatoes peeled and cubed - yield 2 cups
1 cup fresh or frozen cranberries
1 medium onion chopped - yield ½ cup
1 stalk celery cut into pieces
1 clove garlic minced
2 Tablespoons sugar
2 Tablespoons Worcestershire sauce
1½ teaspoon Hungarian paprika
3 juniper berries (optional)
2 whole cloves
1 bay leaf
½ cup cold water
¼ cup rye flour
French bread

In 3 quart saucepan combine venison stew meat with 1½ cups water, salt and pepper. Bring to boil. Reduce heat; cover and simmer 1¼ hours. Stir in wine, carrots, potatoes, cranberries, onions, celery, garlic sugar, Worcestershire sauce, paprika, juniper berries, cloves and bay leaf. Cover and simmer for 45 minutes or until vegetables are tender. Combine the ½ cup cold water and rye flour, stir into stew. Cook and stir until thickened and bubbly. Remove bay leaf. Serve stew with wild rice or French bread.

Makes 6 servings.

Spoehr's Marsh Beef Stew
Home of the famous Walleye spring spawning grounds

5 lbs. of lean venison cut into small pieces
1 quart stock (beef) boiling
1 pint canned tomatoes, chopped
2 cans (12 ounces) beer
3 ounces flour
3 cloves garlic
½ lb. celery cut into ¾ inch pieces
½ lb. onions cut into ¾ inch pieces
3 Tablespoons oil
1 teaspoon thyme
2 bay leaves
1 teaspoon salt
2 teaspoons Worcestershire sauce
½ lb. carrots peeled and cut into ¾ inch pieces
½ lb. potatoes peeled and cut into ¾ inch pieces

Brown venison cubes in oil in a heavy pot. Remove leaving oil in pot. Add onions, celery, and garlic to pot and cook until tender. Place flour in pot, stirring well. Gradually add boiling water or stock and stir until thick and smooth. Add tomatoes, beer, spices and browned venison. Stir until well mixed.

Reduce heat and simmer uncovered 1¼ hours, stirring occasionally. Add carrots and potatoes and cook 30 minutes more, covered.

Makes 12-15 servings.

Marinated - Grilled Venison Roast

Marinade:
- 1 cup salad oil
- ¼ cup lemon juice
- ¼ cup orange juice
- ½ cup red wine vinegar
- 2 Tablespoons A-1 steak sauce
- 2 Tablespoons Worcestershire sauce
- 2 dashes bitters
- 1 small onion, finely chopped
- 2 cloves garlic finely chopped
- 2 Tablespoons soy sauce
- 1 teaspoon lemon pepper
- ½ teaspoon basil leaves, crushed
- 2 bay leaves
- 1 teaspoon Italian seasoning
- 1 teaspoon dried parsley flakes

Mix all ingredients together in a large bowl. Add rolled and tied venison roast. Marinate for 6-8 hours in the refrigerator. Turn venison roast 2-3 times during the marinating process. Use marinade to baste venison roast while cooking on gas or charcoal grill.

VENISON ROAST:
- 8 - 10 lb. venison round (aged for 10 days to 2 weeks)
- 1 lb. sliced bacon
- Cotton string
- Toothpicks
- 2 cups marinade

Trim all excess membrane and fat from aged venison round. Place 5 strips of sliced bacon on the inside of the venison round to be rolled. Roll venison round with the bacon-side in. Tie securely with cotton string. Place in a large bowl with the marinade. Marinate for 6-8 hours in the refrigerator. Turn venison roast 2-3 times during the marinating process. Remove venison roast from the marinade. Wrap remaining sliced bacon strips around the roast; secure with toothpicks. Cook over medium flame of a gas or charcoal grill for about 8 hours or until a meat thermometer inserted in the venison roast registers 160°F internal temperature. Turn and baste venison roast with marinade frequently during the cooking process. After cooking, remove the toothpicks and the bacon strips; discard. Slice the venison roast thin and serve Southern style with hot muffins and butter, coleslaw, and your favorite steamed vegetable.

Makes 6-8 servings.   *Mary T. Weber and William I. Barnes*
Tallahassee, Florida

Indian Jerky

Venison, antelope or elk meat
Salt
Pepper

Salt and pepper the lean strips of venison thoroughly to discourage insects. Then hang the meat over peeled willow poles and dry in the sun. You can also light a smoky chip fire well below the hanging meat and leave it a day or so. Both the sun and fire will dry the strips out. The venison will have a slightly smoky taste. The idea is not to cook the meat, but to dehydrate it.

Wyoming Jerky

Venison or lean meat
Sugar
Seasoning Salt
Pepper
Liquid smoke (optional)

Trim all the fat from the venison. Cut the meat into strips measuring one or two inches wide, a quarter inch thick and six to 10 inches long. Place a layer of the strips in a crock or glass cooking dish. Sprinkle a mixture of three parts sugar, three parts seasoning salt and two parts black pepper. The amount of each ingredient depends on the amount of meat. Sprinkle the mixture on the meat. If you would like a slightly smoky taste, sprinkle on some liquid smoke. Put another layer of meat on top of the first and sprinkle again with seasonings. Repeat this process until all the meat is gone.

Cover the venison and let it stand in a refrigerator for six to eight hours or overnight. After taking the meat out of the refrigerator, cover an oven rack with crushed aluminum foil and evenly space the strips on the foil. Put the rack into an oven no warmer than 150°. Bake until the meat is completely dry, about eight hours.

You can vary the seasoning with herbs salts, such as celery, onion or garlic. For an extra salty taste, before beginning the process, pickle the meat strips in heavy brine for a few hours and then rinse them off.

Air tight jars can be used for storage.

Planked Bear Steak

Trim fat from 2 bear steaks (1½ - 2 inches thick). Marinate in refrigerator for two days, turning several times. Drain, pat dry.

½ **cup butter, melted**
¼ **cup chopped chives**
2 **Tablespoons dijon mustard**
3 **Tablespoons tomato paste**
1 **teaspoon Worcestershire sauce**
1 **clove minced garlic**
Salt and pepper to taste

Cut meat in serving size pieces. Broil meat approximately 6-8 minutes on each side; while basting constantly with the butter and chive mixture.

Makes 4 servings.

Jeannie Geurts
Appleton, Wisconsin

Bear Lunch

(marinated beef, venison or moose/bear stew)

¾ cup cream sherry
2 Tablespoons cooking oil
⅛ teaspoon garlic powder or less to taste
2 lbs. cubed beef, venison, moose or bear meat
¼ cup butter
4 bay leaves
12 peppercorns
12 whole cloves
10 whole allspice
Pepper and seasoned salt to taste
2 beef bouillon cubes
½ cup hot water
2 medium onions, chopped
3 heaping Tablespoons flour
⅓ cup cold water
1 teaspoon vinegar
1 teaspoon sugar
Hot cooked rice or noodles, mashed potatoes or rye bread

In bowl, combine cream sherry, oil and garlic powder. Add meat and toss to coat well. Cover and refrigerate 3-4 days. Stir once or twice while marinating. Drain meat, reserving marinade.

In large, deep skillet over medium high heat, melt and lightly brown butter. Add meat and cook, tossing to brown all sides.

Tie bay leaves, peppercorns, cloves, allspice, pepper and seasoned salt together in cheesecloth bag. Dissolve bouillon cubes in hot water. Place spice bag and bouillon in skillet with meat and onions. Cover and simmer over low heat 1-1½ hours, until meat is fork tender. As juices evaporate, add marinade to keep meat from sticking. When marinade is gone, add water if necessary.

Remove spice bag, and in small bowl combine flour and cold water until smooth. Stir into stew. Cook over medium heat, stirring constantly, until gravy bubbles and is thickened, about 3 minutes. Stir in vinegar and sugar. Serve over rice, noodles, mashed potatoes or rye bread.

Makes 4-6 servings.

Kay Bucholtz

Bear — Hunters' Fashion

The Black Bear who regularly eats and enjoys vegetables, berries, fruit and honey makes for a rich sweet and absolutely delicious meal. It must be hung and marinated. After this, the bear may be cooked like beef steak, except that the neck and hind quarters are too muscular for good eating.

6 lb. piece of loin of bear	6 shallots
¼ lb. larding pork	2 large bay leaves
(cut into strips)	1 large garlic clove
1 quart dry white wine	16 peppercorns
1 cup vinegar	1 Tablespoon salt
2 onions	½ teaspoon dried tarragon
2 carrots	1 cup heavy cream
1 bunch celery	Watercress, lemon, croutons

Lard a 6 lb. piece of bear loin with ¼ lb. larding pork cut into strips. Marinate the meat for 4-5 days in an earthenware crock, turning it from time to time in the marinade.

Mix 1 quart dry white wine and 1 cup vinegar. Add 2 onions and 2 carrots, all sliced, 1 bunch of celery, coarsley chopped, 6 shallots finely chopped, 2 large bay leaves, 1 large garlic clove mashed, 16 peppercorns, 1 Tablespoon salt, and ½ teaspoon dried tarragon. Bring the liquid to a boil, boil it up 3 - 4 times and let it cool.

Strain the marinade and reserve it and put the vegetables into a roasting pan. Put the meat on top of the vegetables and roast the meat in a hot oven — 400° for 15 minutes. Reduce the temperature to moderate — 350° and roast the meat for 1¼ hours loı ger, basting it frequently with the pan drippings. Arrange the meat on a heated platter and keep it hot.

Add 1½ cups strained marinade to the pan drippings, bring it to a boil and reduce it over high heat to 1 generous cup, stirring and scraping the pan to loosen all the brown bits. Add 1 cup scalded heavy cream, bring the sauce to a boil again, and strain it through a fine sieve, pressing gently to extract the vegetable pulp. Over the meat, pour half the sauce and serve the rest in a heated sauceboat. Garnish the platter with watercress, slices of lemon and croutons. Serve with red currant jelly.

Antelope Teriyaki Steak

2 lbs. antelope steak cut thin
1 can beef consommé (undiluted)
⅓ cup soy sauce
1 teaspoon savor salt
2 Tablespoons lemon juice
2 Tablespoons brown sugar
¼ cup chopped green onion (entire onion)
1 clove garlic

Cut the steak diagonally across the grain. Mix other ingredients to form a marinating sauce. Pour the sauce over the meat and refrigerate overnight. Drain and broil 4" from heat until tender.

Serve with wild rice.

Sweet Sour Wild Pig

1 lb. of loin of wild pig or chops cut up. (Soak meat in 3 teaspoons of soy sauce, coat in flour and fry in oil until crisp and brown.)
2 green peppers cut in bite size pieces
1 can (large) of pineapple chunks
1 small can bamboo shoots
1 medium onion cut into bite size pieces
1 medium tomato cut into bite size pieces (optional)

Sauce:
⅔ cup sugar
 8 Tablespoons catsup and or applesauce
 2 Tablespoons wine (red)
 4 Tablespoons vinegar
 8 Tablespoons soy sauce

Fry meat, set aside, cut up and mix vegetables and mix sauce separately.

Put meat and sauce together. Heat and add vegetables. Heat vegetables through. Vegetables should be crisp. Just before serving add ⅔ cup water and 2 Tablespoons of corn starch to entire mix to thicken.

Serve over rice.

Index

To order additional copies of the Wild Game and Country Cookbook, please use the order form below.

Wild Game and Country Cookbook
1212 Nagawicka St.
Delafield, WI 53018

Please send _____ copies of the Wild Game and Country Cookbook at $9.95 each plus $1.50 postage and handling per book. Wisconsin residents add 36¢ sales tax per book.

Send to _____
(Please Print)

Street _____

City _____

State _____ Zip _____

Make Checks Payable to:
The Manion Outdoors Company

Thank You!

Wild Game and Country Cookbook
1212 Nagawicka St.
Delafield, WI 53018

Please send _____ copies of the Wild Game and Country Cookbook at $9.95 each plus $1.50 postage and handling per book. Wisconsin residents add 36¢ sales tax per book.

Send to _____
(Please Print)

Street _____

City _____

State _____ Zip _____

Make Checks Payable to:
The Manion Outdoors Company

Thank You!
